Values in Psychotherapy

CHARLOTTE BUHLER

Values

THE FREE PRESS OF GLENCOE

in Psychotherapy

with a preface by
Edward J. Stainbrook

with contributions by
Rudolf Ekstein
James S. Simkin

and with comments by
George R. Bach
Hedda Bolgar
Zoltan Gross
Fay B. and Maurice J. Karpf
Alvin A. Lasko
Larry Mathae

Foreword

When two or more people come re-
currently together with each other in the social structure and
process of the human encounter called psychotherapy, what,
indeed, does happen? How does it happen? What should
happen? These are the basic questions that challenge the
education of imaginative and experimentally validated answers which will sum up to a science of psychotherapy.

The recent history of psychotherapeutic theory and
practice suggests irresistibly the metaphor of a man running
rapidly backward in order to maintain his visual grasp of an
event expanding too rapidly and too closely in front of him.
But this rapidly increasing conceptual differentiation of the
behavioral situation of psychotherapy can be brought under
rational control by a comprehensive theory of human behavior which does not exclude any relevant aspect of be-
having persons doing some social business together.

This synoptic position in relation to man's behavior has
been achieved by the author of this book. The Faustian

theme of Dr. Charlotte Buhler's intellectual life has been her steadfast devotion to describing, throughout the life-course, the developmental thrust of body and personality, modifying and being modified by the social and cultural conditions that partly define an individual destiny. Within this mature and catholic awareness of what must be seen in human behavior, Dr. Buhler relates the individual learning, unlearning, and relearning as well as the unique creation of human value to the process and outcome of the psycho-therapeutic experience. But further, and importantly, ther-apeutic outcome and experience are considered in relation to the life-style and to the life-stage of the patient.

Clearly, psychotherapy is more than an isolated two-person transaction in a consulting room. As therapist and patient try to intensify to awareness and to understand, from as many meaningful positions as they can conceptualize, the experience they are having with each other, they are, in fact, experiencing each other whether or not all of the ex-perience can be expressed in talk. The two-person encounter is the place where life can be held fast for conceptual re-possession and for prospective revaluation.

But psychotherapeutic practice is also a social institution. Moved by his needs, the patient seeks a role in this social process, which then becomes a part of his current life-style. The life-style at any one time is the total pattern of roles in all the social institutions in which the person participates. Hence, the patient's role behavior in psychotherapy must always be related not only to his internalized past experiences but also to the conditions of his participation in the social institutions of the current life-moment. What any patient, uniquely defined for his present social space, needs from the social process of psychotherapy, what he should have and how he gets it are the most urgent problems for all of us engaged in psychotherapeutic practice.

Dr. Buhler has thought through most of these critical issues clearly and convincingly. The basic theme of the book is a discussion of psychotherapy as value-discrimination, either by reduction of generalization or by new "seeing," but implicit for the reader will be the reward of thinking along with a genuine scholar in the discipline of psychology. Scientific values, like all other values, are not something you have— they are something you do.

EDWARD STAINBROOK, Ph.D., M.D.

Professor and Chairman
Department of Psychiatry
School of Medicine
University of Southern California

Preface

Values are a fairly recent concern of psychology as well as of psychotherapy. Even the concern with goals has only a short scientific history. The reason for this slow approach to problems that seem so central to the study of human behavior and development was the difficulty of finding scientifically acceptable methods.

I, myself, have since the early thirties tried to find techniques to study the human course of life as a psychological problem and have published a first outline of this subject. It represents essentially a study of goals that was approached theoretically as well as by means of biographies. The American edition, which is now in preparation, will add clinical to the biographical material. Some of the considerations and results of this work have been built into the present book.

This book is based on the premise that the study of values in psychotherapy can be handled successfully only if related to the study of values in human life and human development. This volume actually studies two problems: one, the methodological and technical problem whether, why, and how the psychotherapist has to get involved with the value problems of his patient; two, how the therapist's and the patient's self-development and self-understanding and the role that values play for them in human life must by necessity affect the process of therapy.

It is our conviction that values permeate our development and personality to such a degree that they can never be left out of the picture. This book attempts to show this permeating role of values before formulating specific questions of technique.

At this point, I should perhaps state my present theoretical position as clearly as I am able to. My original studies on different phases of human development were based essentially on *behavioristic* principles of overt behavior observations on the one hand, and on *introspective* methods, as they were developed in the Würzburg school of thought processes on the other. The data that we assembled, remained entirely within the realm of *observable activities* and/or conscious experiences. I did not think at the time that motivation could be approached as yet successfully.

In the meantime, Freud of course proved that it could be done. My difficulties with the theoretical system of *psychoanalysis* were, however, considerable. To start with, Freud's *pan-sexualism* and his totalitarian *pleasure principle* impressed me as out of all proportion. When from Adler, Jung, Rank and then particularly from different quarters in the American development of psychoanalysis remedies for this bias were introduced, I still did not see that they made the system valid.

One remedy was the replacement of the pleasure principle with the *homeostasis*—or discharge principle which Freud himself had already proposed. I still could not see that this was a solution, because I find myself in agreement with the criticism starting from Kurt Goldstein and finding recent expression by Thomas Szasz, that homeostasis is not a goal of the organism, but only a condition to which it always tries to return from disturbances as well as from what its real goals are, namely accomplishments. Strangely enough, some analysts, such as R. R. Grinker, can describe brilliantly the *built-in tension* in the organism and then still go on, as if nothing were changed with the rest of the system.

For me everything is changed by the concept of built-in tension, because it means that beyond tension and release of tension, we have to look for what the goals are instead. Here is where the *self-realization*—or *self-actualization*—*theory* comes in.

These theories—which were introduced by Karen Horney, Erich Fromm, and Kurt Goldstein, and which were recently shown in their application to normal development by Abraham Maslow—had their enormous appeal and found wide acceptance in America because they provided what psychoanaylsis was lacking in: *accomplishment* of the self seen as a primary goal with a new consideration of the realities of different backgrounds, social and cultural conditions.

With these systems, I feel great affinity and I could have identified with them, were it not again for certain shortcomings that I found myself unable to accept.

I see positive aspects of these theories in that they work with a *positive reality* principle, that they give *creativity* a basic role, that they introduce the principle of *accomplishment* on a primary instead of a superego basis, and that with all that, they put the truly human aspects of life into the foreground. Furthermore, they rebuke the false value of the "adjustment to society" ideal, which was often read into the Freudian theory and which they have shown to be invalid in view of most societies' deficiencies.

However, there are unfortunately, also negative aspects. First of all, these theories have, while they gained the consideration for the role of social and cultural backgrounds, lost more or less completely the connection with the *biogenetic* factors of life. With this I feel, they lost the ground under their feet. While talking about self-realization, they do not attempt to study *human development* in its concrete aspects of dispositions and learning, maturational sequences of functions and behavior, the actual role of *potentialities* and limitations and so on. The latter has been attempted by Abraham Maslow to the degree that he investigated self-realizing individuals' development.

A second shortcoming is that the postulates of these theories have not been thought through in terms of their *scientific premises*. Reality is assumed to be positive, creativity assumed to be primary, accomplishment assumed to be a basic tendency, but none of this is proved in scientific terms.

A third shortcoming, I see in the *totally holistic* approach. While I am in full accord with the postulate that the individual is a whole and represents a unit, which acts as such and has over-all goals concerning this whole, I consider it an oversimplification to do away with all subdivisions of this whole. To me there is no doubt that Freud's *triad system* of id, ego, and superego has its irreplaceable merits, particularly for the understanding of conflicting trends within the personality. I feel it ought to be worked into a theory of what the whole does, instead of being left out of it.

Finally, there remains a word to be said about the modern *ego psychology*. The new ego psychology, which finds much acclaim and is being developed in many quarters, also tries to remedy certain disparities of earlier pyschoanalytic theorizing. The ego-psychologists try to place the one-sided emphasis on unconscious processes with a stronger acknowledgment of the importance of *conscious* experiences.

This brings them closer to developmental and functional psychology as it used to be before analysis came into the picture. But only to a degree.

They come close to a *positive reality concept,* which developmentalists used in a naive sort of way. But as analysts they have to justify it. Here is Heinz Hartmann's important contribution. Hartmann tries to circumscribe an area or an experiential realm in which reality can be positive and experienced conflict-free. However, how can he do it without bringing accomplishment down to the ground floor? Perception and movement are adaptive and creative accomplishments, they are not undertaken for the sake of homeostasis. They are play in the beginning, but they later become purposeful actions with goals that require the overcoming of difficulties; thus only by forcing an issue, could they be subsumed under the category of pleasure seeking. So how can the pleasure principle and the positive reality principle jibe?

Another difficulty is the *exclusive emphasis on the ego-factor* in these processes; this is alien to our previous procedures and brings them, in my opinion, under an unduly narrowing and confining perspective. In its naively holistic outlook, developmental psychology left things open for clarification in further research. In the present ego-psychology, it is all settled, all observable behavior and all that is conscious experience has to be ego, because it is neither id nor superego.

But what about the *self?* While the representatives of the self-realization theory have not reasoned it out, their theory leads to the logical conclusion that the self processes, which underlie everything, also permeate everything. In my second chapter, I have discussed this in considerable detail. I think much in the way Horney did, that our true or distorted self directs our conscious thinking. I also think that it is quite possible to separate the manifestations of this self from the ego-concerns. Although this has, to my knowledge not as yet been attempted in any concrete case study and with theoretical discrimination.

This whole self-system as we must obviously see it—I agree with Munroe's criticism of Horney's self as an entitity—needs clarification for what it is. Here is where Erik Erikson's work on self-processes comes in. It gives us colorful and concrete pictures of them. However, the relationship of Erikson's self concept and the ego still remain unclear to me, as does the system of categories on which his self-development is built.

Thus, I had to think things through in my own way trying to profit from the immense body of knowledge that the different analytic schools had placed before us in the last decades.

Again, I have had the assistance of many friends whose advice and comments I acknowledge with gratitude. Hedda Bolgar, Rudolf Ekstein, and James S. Simkin had the kindness to read my whole manuscript and to give me the benefit of their experience. Their own contribution to this book I consider a great asset. Next I want to thank all the participants of my Value Study Group whose discussions of this controversial subject of values in psychotherapy helped me to clarify my own ideas. Specifically, I want to thank those who contributed formulated comments. They are George Bach, Hedda Bolgar, Zoltan Gross, Fay B. and Maurice J. Karpf, Alvin A. Lasko, and Larry Mathae. Comments on various points of my presentation were given by Bernice Eiduson, Fred Hacker, and Zelda Wolpe. I got much encouragement from Gordon Allport and Abraham Maslow. As always, my husband Karl Buhler assisted me all through the book. Irreplaceable was also James S. Simkin's kind help in the function of an excellent, never-tiring editor. Dr. Heinz Hartmann was kind enough to read the manuscript of this book and to further the clarification of our two theoretical positions.

Since Dr. Edward Stainbrook was willing to write a foreword, I received the assurance that it was sound from both the psychological as well as the psychiatric points of view.

Finally, I want to thank the Free Press, particularly Mr. Jeremiah Kaplan, Mrs. Barbara Fried, and Mr. W. W. Schmitt for the interest they expressed in my book.

CHARLOTTE BUHLER, Ph.D.

Los Angeles, June, 1961.

Affiliations

Charlotte Buhler, Ph.D.
Formerly Associate Professor of Psychology, University of Vienna
Emerita Assistant Clinical Professor of Psychiatry, University of Southern
California School of Medicine, Los Angeles, Calif.
Private Practice, Beverly Hills, Calif.

Edward J. Stainbrook, M.D., Ph.D.
Professor and Chairman, Department of Psychiatry, University of
Southern California School of Medicine
Chief Psychiatrist, Los Angeles County General Hospital

Rudolf Ekstein, Ph.D.
Coordinator of Training and Research at the Reiss Davis Clinic for
Child Guidance, Los Angeles, Calif.
Instructor, the Los Angeles Institute for Psychoanalysis

James S. Simkin, Ph.D.
Private Practice, Beverly Hills, Calif.
Visiting Assistant Professor, Los Angeles State College
Parent Education Teacher, Los Angeles School System
Psychotherapist, Westwood Community Methodist Church Mental
Hygiene Clinic

George R. Bach, Ph.D.
Director, Institute of Group Psychotherapy, Beverly Hills, Calif.
Lecturer, Claremont Graduate School, Claremont, Calif.

Hedda Bolgar, Ph.D.
Chief Psychologist and Director, Clinical Psychology Training Program,
Psychiatric and Psychosomatic Research Institute, Mount Sinai
Hospital, Los Angeles, Calif.

Zoltan Gross, Ph.D.
Private Practice, Beverly Hills, Calif.

Fay B. Karpf, Ph.D.
Formerly Faculty Member and Student Research Director, The Graduate
School for Jewish Social Work, New York City
Private Practice, Beverly Hills, Calif.

Maurice J. Karpf, Ph.D.
Formerly Professor of Social Technology and President of the Faculty,
The Graduate School for Jewish Social Work, New York City
Private Practice, Beverly Hills, Calif.

Alvin A. Lasko, Ph.D.
Formerly Assistant Professor of Psychology, University of California,
Los Angeles
Co-Director Psychological Services
Co-Director Psychological Service Associates, Los Angeles, Calif.

Larry Mathae, Ph.D.
Chief Clinical Psychologist, Griffin Clinic
Private Practice, Encino, Calif.

Contents

Values in Psychotherapy

Introduction: The Problem
of Values in Psychotherapy

1.
The Problem

One cannot live without encountering the problem of values. Certainly, one cannot go through psychotherapy without becoming involved, implicitly or explicitly, in the problem. Nor can one engage in psychotherapy as a therapist without bringing certain convictions about values into one's work. These convictions may or may not be specifically communicated to the patient, but they underlie the therapist's activity; they help determine the goal he sets for himself and his patient; and they are consciously or unconsciously reflected in his questions, statements, or other reactions.

In spite of their all-pervading presence, values were

formerly not a concern of the psychotherapist except insofar as they revealed information about the patient's neurotic drives. The information revealed was what the therapist focused on, not the values as such. The conflicts among and distortions of values were expected to straighten out as the patient matured in the handling of his drives.

Only very recently have we come to realize that there are more psychologically relevant issues involving values than their being healthy or distorted projections. We have come to see that different value systems exist and that the choice of a particular value system exposes a person to problems and conflicts that are not necessarily of a neurotic origin. Instead, these problems and conflicts result from beliefs and convictions that arise from different interpretations of human life.

The existence of these problems has been acknowledged recently in an increasing number of publications. In these publications it is pointed out that *patients* come into therapy with *values acquired in a specific background* from which arise problems relating to the interpretation of human life. We, however, take note of these problems only incidentally as they are reflected in the patient's struggle with his drives. The reason for this incidental notice lies, of course, in the concept and techniques of psychotherapy.

In the recent literature, for example in works by Redlich (1953, 1957) and Opler (1956), attention has been called to the existence of problems relating to background and to the not infrequent misinterpretation of patients' beliefs as symptoms. Spiegel and his collaborators (1959) demonstrated in their studies that the knowledge of the patient's *Weltanschauung* and background made a difference in the patient-therapist relationship.

2

In Spiegel's study and other studies as well, equal atten-tion has been directed to the *value system of the therapist* as a corresponding frame of reference within which he functions without necessarily having clarified for himself just how his values affect his procedure and his impact on the patient.

While these first two points have already come rather clearly into focus, a third point still remains completely unclarified. It is the question of *how (between patient and therapist) values are actually communicated,* and, further, *how values should be handled in the patient-therapist rela-tionship.* Officially, it is only the patient who talks about his values. And, officially, all he gets in response are inter-pretive remarks and questions. But is this actually so?

An increasing amount of literature, of which examples will be quoted later, cites evidence of the fact that, knowingly or unknowingly, *the therapist conveys to the patient some of his thinking about values.* This seems to be the case even in the most nondirective, or seemingly purely interpretive, approaches. It seems that the therapist conveys to the patient something beyond his understanding of the patient's moti-vation struggles. He reveals, knowingly or unknowingly, on rare or more frequent occasions his own personal *reaction,* his *point of view,* or even his *position* in matters of conse-quence. And of course he cannot help revealing, beyond the technically acquired model, attitudes of "poise, patience, fairness, consistency, rationality, kindliness, in short—his *real* love for the patient" (Menninger, 1958), some of his own personality characteristics.

For those who acknowledge the validity of these findings, what follows is the recognition of the fact that human beings cannot engage in the development of what amounts to a very important relationship and avoid, or pretend to avoid, the evolving of an *understanding about some basic principles of living.* Or if they do, little therapy takes place; for this statement casuistic evidence can be supplied.

In other words, the therapeutic relationship becomes an effective *human* impact through the undercurrent of human values that both the therapist and the patient feel to be of the essence in their lives; while the therapeutic relationship becomes an effective *emotional* impact through the analysis of motivation.

What do we now know about this human impact in terms of methods? Its existence is acknowledged in technical terms under the aspects of "transference" and of "identification."

Transference is basically conceived of as an unconsciously distorted impact resulting from the patient's emotional involvements and misapprehensions. It is destined to be resolved, not to remain. Whatever remains from it in the forms of affection and friendship is incidental, not programmatic. Identification is handled within the framework of psychoanalysis and psychotherapy as something that, hopefully, will come about in the right way, but not as something that is induced by a specific method.

Let us look, for example, at Ekstein's (1956) summarizing statement about the process that takes place in analysis, which he schematically demonstrates in an interesting model.

He describes the two movements through which "the hypothetical ideal ego" goes at the same time:

> One is regressive, the transference neurosis; and the other, progressive, leading to a strengthening and maturing of previously unavailable ego functions. The hypothetical ideal ego then experiences a "mild split" (L. Stone), consisting of regressive transference features, which lead to identification

4

with the analytic task, and progressive interpretive features relating to the analyst's function of finding an ally in the mature aspects of the patient's ego. In our ideal patient, there is a perfect correlation of regressive and progressive features which will lead to an expansion of the self-organization in both directions, the appropriate availability of primitive (originally repressed) functions as well as mature (not originally available) functions of the ego. The transference neurosis, a primarily archaic relationship, will finally be dissolved, and will give way to a mature object relationship to the analyst (p. 81).

In accord with psychoanalytic theory, Ekstein sees the progressive development of the mature, previously not utilized functions of the ego as a result of interpretive techniques successfully used.

The expectations regarding the functioning of this more mature ego have been spelled out by Karl Menninger (1958) in an admirably comprehensive description. He gives a vivid picture of the rounded, healthily functioning person who has achieved a "sense of greater freedom, a capacity for more joy in life, a cessation of various compulsive activities and a diminution of the tendency to depression" (p. 166). There is only one point in Menninger's description in which the conclusions are not completely definitive nor the details comprehensive, that is with respect to the functioning of the patient's value system.

The reason seems to be—and this is also indicated by Menninger—that it is not completely clear how the patient's identity and new value system proceed from analysis. Analysis and psychotherapy may help a patient to inner freedom and self-understanding, but do they help him to believe in the meaning of human existence and in a purpose to his own life if history, science, and/or his own experiences and observations make these beliefs doubtful to him? According to Freud himself, psychoanalysis does not purport to lead to a *Weltanschauung*. It assumes that the freed patient can find it himself.

Here, of course, is where the teachings of existentialism enter. Frankl's logotherapy specifically develops in his patients the "will to meaning." That is, he supplements or even replaces analysis with teaching.

The main question raised in this book is whether between the extreme of *leaving the patient to find his values and beliefs himself* through his capacity for identification or whatever other methods his freed and strengthened ego allows him to develop, and the other extreme of *actively inducing beliefs in him* (in switching to the role of an educator)—whether between these two extremes there are not other possibilities. This question will be discussed at length and research ideas will be suggested.

There is, however, a second, perhaps even more valid reason for the study of this whole problem area—because this second reason refers to a source of more frequently occurring problems: the incident of *indecision based on the uncertainties of our present culture's value system*. In a culture that to a great extent has lost its unifying beliefs and convictions, even persons with stronger egos and better judgment than some of our patients could ever muster may feel stymied when it comes to certain basic decisions, decisions about right and wrong in matters of personal, sex, and family life involving situations like divorce, extra- and premarital intercourse, birth control, handling of authority, discipline, and so forth.

While I do not think that many therapists would feel that switching from the role of therapist to that of educator is a satisfactory solution, there seem to be intermediate possibilities of intervention. These additional possibilities will be discussed in later chapters.

2.

Historical Review

The problem of exactly what the therapist conveys to his patients in his questions and interpretations is one that is of the greatest concern to many clinicians of our time.

Rogers' originally "nondirective" approach (1951) to psychotherapy was prompted by his concern that the patient should remain autonomous in his development and direction.

Historically speaking, we can, I believe, distinguish three periods. First, Freud himself and some of his earlier pupils (such as Richard C. Sterba, Franz Alexander, Melitta Schmideberg, Edward Bibring, and others) speak of "pedagogic measures" that have to be used, "to press the patient into a new decision" as Freud says. Ferenczy, who suggested the "active" technique of psychoanalysis, also uses a degree of "pedagogic guidance." Sterba (1944) quotes both in full agreement. Alexander (1958) has recently considered this whole area of the psychoanalyst's influence as highly problematic. He calls it "the most opaque area of psychoanalysis." Melitta Schmideberg, on the other hand, has recently (1961) summarized in a systematic manner her repeatedly publicized position in regard to a rather active guiding approach. We will later return to some of her thoughtful considerations.

Edward Glover (1958), whom Sterba considers to be in agreement with the "active" approach, expresses himself, however, in his comprehensive volume, *The Technique of Psychoanalysis*, as actually against active techniques. In fact,

7

he deplores the "abandonment of neutrality" as "the main disadvantage inherent in active methods" (p. 175).

This, then, is characteristic of a second period of psycho-analysis and psychotherapy. *Neutrality, detachment,* and *non-interference* seem characteristic of the psychoanalytic technique of this period. In the nonanalytically oriented psycho-therapeutic groups, Rogers' nondirective method emphasized an even greater abstinence from intervention by the therapist.

At present, in what we may call the third period, Rogers himself, as well as other psychotherapists of varying orientation and certain groups of psychoanalysts, tends to reintroduce more active and participating procedures.

There are actually three different reasons for this wide-spread new tendency. The first is that *consciously* or *unconsciously* the therapist conveys his opinions. The second is that the unnaturalness of "the analyst's anonymity" and "ivory tower" is being criticized. The third is that there is uncertainty about values in our time. Consequently, the patient may need help in finding valid values, and he should be reassured that different positions in matters of values can be taken and are acceptable.

Some examples of these three considerations may be given. In respect to the first point, the therapist's conscious and, more frequently, unconscious conveying of subjective *opinions* under the guise of interpretation has already been criticized by Richard Sterba (1944). In criticizing the "abuse of interpretation" he speaks initially about extra-analytic situations. But he extends his reference to the "striking want of psychoanalytic common sense" in "so many analysts" (p. 11) in their "wild" interpretations within the analytic situation itself. Sterba feels that certain personal needs of the analyst are responsible for this behavior. On

8

the other hand, Sterba is perhaps one of the most outspoken representatives of the view that the analyst should exercise an educational influence on the analysand. This will be discussed further on (see pp. 18 ff.).

The fact that the analyst might communicate his views "by implication" was brought out in Edward Glover's (1958) careful and detailed studies of the technique of interpretation, although the majority of the respondents to a research-study questionnaire by Glover expressed themselves to be against conscious statements of opinions at any rate.

The lack of unanimity in the use of the analytic technique and the prominent role of the analyst's personal judgment in these matters becomes evident in Glover's finding that only six points of technique are "almost" completely agreed upon by twenty-four psychoanalysts and that there are seventy-six further points on which there exists a division of opinion. One of these points is "communication of analyst's personal opinions."

The extraordinary degree to which this expression of opinions in direct form or "by implication" actually takes place in pyschoanalysis as well as in psychotherapy, is brought to light in some of the current tape-recorded studies. A statement made by Hedda Bolgar in reference to the research-study material collected on tape at Mount Sinai Hospital in Los Angeles under Franz Alexander may be repeated here.[1] In a personal communication she said:

> Psychoanalysts and other psychotherapists are often unaware how large a portion of each analytic session is devoted to the exchange of values between the therapist and the patient. Into each analysis, the patient brings with him the values of his own social and cultural group which he has

---

1. This study is in preparation for publication.

internalized, sometimes in pure form, sometimes distorted. Frequently, he brings his search for values by which he can live more successfully. The analyst also brings the values of his own social and cultural group as he has internalized them. In addition, more or less integrated with the social values, he brings the value system of psychoanalysis. *This value system and the analyst's personal interpretation of it, is the basis of most of his interventions in the course of therapy* [italics mine]. It is true—analysts, by and large, refrain from moral judgments of good and bad, but it is not always easy to enforce the "fundamental rule" without conveying to the patient that it is "bad" to withhold associations or to control feelings or to edit the words that come to mind. It is equally difficult to work toward a change in the patient without implying that some or much about him at present is "bad." Much of what is taught the patient by whatever techniques the analyst's skill and tact provide, may be unacceptable to the patient. Often, what is called "resistance" in psychoanalysis, is rather conscious rejection of the analyst's values and conversely much of the patient's "insight" or "growth" is the direct result of his acceptance of the analyst's values. Ultimately, a successful analysis may not depend on the patient's ability or willingness to accept the analyst's values unchanged. In the process of evaluating and re-evaluating the analyst's values as well as his own, he may indeed arrive at a new value system of his own.

In a similar vein, Edward Glover (1958) points out that the analyst's "refusal to admit the reality of some of the patient's observations" may "lead to theoretical distortion or to actual overemphasis of phantasy interpretations" (p. 312).

In reference to the unnaturalness of the "analyst's anonymity," Sol W. Ginsburg and J. L. Herma (1953) declare: "The analyst who feels strongly motivated by social values cannot turn aside from such activities without undermining his own integrity and feelings of self-esteem and any such denial might well affect his relationships with his patients, certainly as much and more so than mere compliance with a technical rule" (p. 558). This study is of particular interest not only because of the authors' stimulating presentation of many value aspects of psychotherapy, but also because of a number of important points brought out in the discussion following the presentation of this paper.

All participants in the discussion agreed that the therapist's values influence the patient. Some speakers went much further and declared, like Jon Ehrenwald, that the therapist "must help the patient evolve and fortify a system of values which stands up to the criteria of reality testing and is, at the same time, based on the patient's cultural background and personal experience. The therapist should not try to convert the patient to his—the therapist's philosophy and system of values" (p. 568).

William Wolf said: "In therapy, then, we can make use of value judgments, by helping the patient place high values upon what is attainable to him at the moment, what is congruous with his personality, what makes for survival, happiness, time binding sense of achievement or peace of mind, and low value or stress upon the opposites" (p. 571).

This confirms then what Gordon Allport remarks (1956):

> Sometimes we hear it said that psychoanalytic theory does not do justice to psychoanalytic practice. What is meant is that in the course of therapy an analyst will devote much of his time to a direct discussion with his patient of his manifest interests and values. The analyst will listen respectfully, accept, counsel, and advise concerning these important, and *not* buried, psychodynamic systems. In many instances, as in the cases presented by Kardiner and Ovesey, the motives and conflicts are taken at their face value. Thus the method of psychoanalysis as employed is not fully sustained by the theory that is affirmed (p. 35).

Werner Wolff (1956), who made an intensive interview

study of forty-four New York psychotherapists and psycho-analysts of the leading schools, found that according to 48 per cent, "value concepts of the therapist do have and should have a direct influence upon the therapy"; according to 24 per cent an indirect influence was stated. Only 28 per cent denied this factor.

In addition, 60 per cent of those interviewed believed that the personality of the therapist is an "important factor" in therapy.

In conclusion, Wolff states that there is a "growing emphasis on action and directiveness in therapeutic attitudes."

Very frequently the analyst and the analysand engage, consciously or unconsciously, in experiences and interchanges stemming from the value-concept relationship that are not dealt with in the textbooks. Such experiences have important impacts. Comparative studies of patients' recovery and further development after receiving treatment with or without this type of intervention are greatly needed.

A thoughtful statement by Gardner Murphy (1955) in answer to the question: "Shall personnel and guidance work . . . attempt to impart a philosophy of life?" is quoted by C. H. Patterson (1959), in a new textbook, *Counseling and Psychotherapy*.

While admitting that "no one knows enough to construct an adequate philosophy of life," Murphy says that, "nevertheless if he who offers guidance is a whole person, with real roots in human culture, he cannot help conveying directly or indirectly to every client what he himself sees and feels, and the perspective in which his own life is lived."

The questions that arise are obvious. They concern first of all, the problem of the individual counselor's maturity and wisdom, and secondly, the problem of procedure. Little research has been done as yet as to when and how opinions should be stated. It could hardly be considered desirable that we return in this matter to an arbitrary and haphazard procedure after so many careful considerations have been given to methods of interpretation.

Before further discussion of these two questions, some authors may be quoted with respect to the previously mentioned third reason that might prompt the discussion of value problems in present-day psychotherapy, the fact of *our times' uncertainty regarding the validity of many transmitted values.*

This problem is emphasized by Allen Wheelis (1958) who discusses the "basic trouble about value" as "an urgent problem of our time" (p. 174). The "collapse of values" and the general uncertainty in the field of value lead "patients to apply" to their analysts "for values which analysis cannot provide" (p. 188).

The urging of the consideration of value aspects in psychotherapy is most thoroughly emphasized by existential analysts whose viewpoint has found an echo in the writings of prominent American psychologists such as Rollo May (1958).

A re-evaluation of our therapeutic value concepts is recommended by O. H. Mowrer (1960) and T. S. Szasz (1960), who both debate the validity of our present concept of "mental illness."

The problems arising out of the existence of divergent value systems was mentioned in the first part of this introduction, while quoting the studies of several social psychiatrists. C. Marshal Lowe (1959) tries to categorize four separate and discrete value orientations, which he calls: "naturalism" (defined as the value of obtaining physical comfort); "culturalism" (defined as the value of social adaptation); "humanism" (defined as the value of self-sufficiency and self-realization); and "theism" (defined as the value of submission to and love of God).

Lowe feels that "the dilemma of the practicing psychologist is compounded by the existence of a multiplicity of competing sets of values, for one value orientation tends to exclude all others." He further concludes that these differences in value orientation cannot be resolved and suggests that each therapist, ". . . have an understanding of the values both of himself and others and that his values be known by all who are personally affected by his professional behavior."

An impressive attempt to arrive at a system of value orientation by a comparative study has been made by Charles Morris (1956a–1956c). In studying and analyzing the value orientations of seven different religions, Morris finds "thirteen conceptions of the good life" or thirteen *ways to live*," which are emphasized to different degrees in different religions and cultures. They appear in three main patterns that Morris calls *basic components of the human personality*: "dionysian" (defined as "tendencies to release and indulge existing desires"); "promethean" (defined as "active tendencies to manipulate and remake the world"); and "buddhist" (defined as "tendencies in the self to regulate itself by holding in check its desires").

After having several hundred students of Eastern as well as Western cultures rate these "ways" in terms of preferences, Morris comes to the conclusion that there is a striking "stability over the various regions of a given culture" (1956, p. 69).

Recently the "ways" were studied by Morris, Eiduson, and O'Donovan (1960) with a sample of psychiatric out-patients

14

of the Hacker Foundation for Psychiatric Research and Education, and their ratings were compared with a control group. Some of the findings will be discussed in Chapter 3.

Marshall Lowe and Charles Morris' analyses of basic value orientations have certain aspects in common, and the different basic trends that they distinguish are to a great extent also consistent with the author's theory of four basic tendencies of life.

The theory of four basic tendencies of life was developed by the author (1959c) as a result of quite different considerations than those of Lowe and Morris. Lowe compared the views of different clinicians in regard to their therapeutic goals; Morris compared the values pursued in different religions and cultures; I, on the other hand, studied present-day biological thinking and present-day psychological theorizing on basic tendencies of life. After a critical survey I came to the conclusion that the following four tendencies could not further be reduced: "need-satisfaction" (defined as tendencies toward release, comfort, happiness); "self-limiting adaptation" (defined as tendencies toward restriction, fitting-in, security); "expansive creativity" (defined as tendencies toward expansion, creativity, self-realization); and "upholding of the internal order" (defined as tendencies toward integration, self-sustenance, peace of mind). It is hypothesized that at all times all tendencies are present in every individual, but that they manifest themselves in individually and developmentally varying distributions.

All three theories (those of Lowe, Morris, and the author) have three factors in common. They distinguish what they call the tendency to psychophysical comfort, self-restriction, and self-realization in creativity.

Only the fourth factor is seen differently. Morris does

15

not include the fourth factor in his system because he interprets self-restriction as an implement to self-regulation, while Lowe and the author interpret self-restriction as being related to social adaptation. This factor of wanting to fit oneself into the universe and society and feel one belongs, is to my mind a basic component of Judaeo-Christian culture. In Morris' system this "wanting to fit in" and to belong does not appear as a basic component, although his "way 1" actually describes just this desire.

The tendency to what might be called sustenance of the self in terms not of self-sufficiency but of inner strength and peace of mind is attributed by Morris to self-restriction. I am inclined to relate this peace of mind—self-sustenance to inner order, while Lowe relates it to religion; that is, in his terms it is a submission and love relationship with God.

In spite of these disparities, the three attempts have enough in common to warrant the therapist's consideration of the fact that basically different value orientations are held by individual patients and therapists alike. There must be room for the consideration of this fact in psychotherapy. But how?

To my knowledge only the previously mentioned textbook, *Counseling and Psychotherapy*, discusses the problem of values in psychotherapy comprehensively. While it raised more questions than it answers, C. M. Patterson's (1959) book deserves more detailed consideration.

To my knowledge, he raises the problems that we introduced more fully than any other psychological clinician has. He discusses the value problem from all three aspects that I introduced at the beginning of this study, and he takes a rather definite stand with respect to them.

First, he feels that the client-centered therapy that he

promotes is based in itself on a value system. Its two main theses are "that each person is a person of worth in himself and is therefore to be respected as such," and, secondly, "that each individual has the right of self-direction, to choose or select his own values and goals and to make his own decisions" p. 57). This value naturally is not limited to the nondirective school.

Secondly, he brings evidence from a number of studies proving an actual influence exercised by the therapist on "the patient's values without attempting to do so or being aware of it" (p. 67).

And, thirdly, he expresses the opinion that since "the counselor"'s moral attitudes and values do enter into counseling . . . it prevents the counselor from erroneously believing that he is neutral" if he expresses his own opinions freely. However, he should clearly label them as his own values and opinions and allow the patient to feel free to choose his own.

Patterson concludes his chapter with this advice to counselor-students: that the therapist should be himself in his relationships with the client. This he quotes as Rogers' more recent point of view, too, a fact representing a remarkable change in Rogers' technique.

Here is where the problem of techniques arises. While Patterson distinguishes between the counselor's expression of his own convictions and the counselor's direct attempt to influence his patient, Richard Sterba in an early paper (1944) advocates a direct postinterpretive educational influence that the analyst should exercise on his analysand.

The patient, he says, is apt to fall back into previous patterns of behavior due to "mental inertia." Also, he may not find a way to apply the newly acquired knowledge about

17

himself. Sterba speaks of pedagogic measures, or the "formative activity" of the analyst, to establish the reorientation of the patient's personality in actual life. In fact, Sterba goes so far as to declare that we should use the patient's "respect for our opinion" in order to "mould" him "into a healthier personality formation." Sterba quotes Freud's statement that we must use "all our available mental forces in order to press the patient into a new decision." He also quotes Franz Alexander as being among the few who admit an "active influence of the analyst upon the assimilation process going on within the patient."

Sterba feels that this "formative activity is a part of our work which can hardly be learned and for which we can give neither prescription nor technical advice." It is truly creative and in it the personality of the analyst becomes the "decisive factor."

In a very recent paper (1960), Sterba discusses the problem of the therapeutic goal in the light of present-day reality. He feels that present-day reality creates even greater problems of coping with personal feelings as well as with feelings toward values, than was the case in Freud's time. He says, much in the vein of his previous ideas on guidance:

> "What am I supposed to feel?" is a frequent question of our patients. It then becomes our therapeutic task to give the patient an orientation in the world of feelings, to provide or at least to demonstrate a framework of structures for recognition of and contact with their feelings, and to make the pathways of emotional discharge available to them. With some patients, it is necessary to describe minutely the different possibilities of feeling reactions, which are to be expected as responses to stimuli, almost to feel them for them as a demonstration so that they can orient themselves in the world of emotions, so estranged have their egos become from these heretofore most natural responses (p. 215).

The point under debate here is this: Do we have to leave this fundamental question of influences exercised on a patient to the decisions and wisdom of the individual therapist? Sterba resigns himself to this necessity; Patterson does not see a problem necessarily arising from the question being left in the hands of the individual analyst, nor do Ginsburg and the previously quoted discussants of his paper. I, personally, have always felt that this question of influences is a tremendous problem, and so do many clinical psychologists with whom I have discussed the issue.

Clinical psychologists and psychologically trained counselors are currently particularly alert to the problem of the extent of *adequate intervention* by the therapist. The conveying of opinions, viewpoints, and values is by and large regarded with disfavor, although the issue is debated.

3.
Study Group on Values[2]

In discussions with therapists, one finds them applying a number of completely different principles to this area of the therapeutic situation. Some therapists have not given the matter any specific thought; others feel that "a patient loses faith if you don't take any stand in psychotherapy"; and others are of the opinion that the therapist should remain impersonal and uncommitted at all times. This, however, does not mean that the patient interprets the therapist's air of impersonality in the way in which it is intended. He may, as E. A. Loomis (1959) points out, react to the silence

---

2. In November, 1958, the author founded in Los Angeles a "Study Group on Values in Psychotherapy." Some of the subsequent statements refer to comments made during these sessions, and are made with the permission of the speakers.

as if the therapist means to consent to what he is doing, or he may feel that the therapist is cold and disinterested, and so forth.

But if and inasmuch as the therapist takes a stand, how does this affect his patient? The patient may experience the therapist as an authority whose views on life he himself should adopt; he may feel hostile to his therapist for not sharing his prejudices; or he may try to begin arguing and debating opinions.

I remember in this connection the puzzled question of a young psychologist to whom a very capable student-patient complained that he could never make A's in his final grades. "What stand should I take?" asked the young therapist. "Do I say 'why can't you make A's?' or do I say 'Why should you make A's?' "

The colleagues he asked told him: "There is a third question that you can ask your patient—without taking a stand yourself, that is, 'Why is it important to you to make A's?' " They could also have suggested that he ask about the origin of his patient's feelings of never living up to his or somebody else's expectations. These questions would lead the patient to think about his motivation on a deeper level in a new way rather than make him repeat thoughts he was more likely to have gone through before himself. The therapist said, yes, he could see that, and he wished in his training such principles had been discussed. He was never sure when to indicate his stand on things and when not.

Whoever taught him might easily have given him the principle of going on as long as possible exploring the patient's motives, rather than asking questions in which his own opinions were intimated. But the point might still have come where the patient might have said, "O.K., so now I

20

want to make A's because I want to prove at least to my father that I can make them if I want to—but now tell me *your* opinion of A's. Do you think one should invest the energy to try to make them, if one has to work hard for them, or is it not worth it?"

The therapist might again avoid taking a stand and might ask whether the patient thought his further career in college and after would be favorably affected by the A's, and so forth. But at some point the patient might have insisted on having the therapist's opinion on the questions: Should one always try one's best, should one give one's utmost to work, or should one just do enough to get by and pursue other goals?

At this point the therapist might or might not take a personal stand. He might say that this is a matter of personal opinion, of a person's philosophy of life, or he might say, that he, himself, would invest his energies primarily in what seemed most important to him and so on.

Perhaps the therapist's stand on this matter would not make too much difference. But there are other situations in which his opinion could have a tremendous impact. Some such examples will be discussed in later chapters. The point is: Should the decision be left to the therapist's judgment, skill, and personal inclination? Or, should alternative solutions be studied and become part of our training?

When the example of the student who wanted to make A's was discussed in the above mentioned Value Study Group, Dr. James S. Simkin expressed himself as opposed to taking any stand at all:

> In my opinion, the therapist, in taking a "personal stand," uses a defensive maneuver as a result of feeling threatened by the patient at this point. I feel it is a technical mistake if

21

the therapist forces his own values on the patient under the guise of "education." Even though in a few instances I gave in to my own needs to voice an opinion, I consider this my own weakness. And my principle is that such statements should be generally avoided, and the patient should be left to find his own values.[3]

Dr. George Bach expressed a different opinion:

Concerning the therapist's communication to his patients of his own values by which he lives, my clinical experience shows this can be of great service, provided, however, that the patient is actively prevented from using such information to avoid finding his own identity by imitation. I share more of my own striving for and struggle with values and goal-structuring, especially in the area of the patients' concerns, than my final value commitments. Furthermore, I stress that my ways of wrestling with value problems are to be taken only as a reference point to gain perspective, to compare, rather than to imitate. As a technical general rule, I reinforce and stress *self-differentiating* experiences in therapy (especially group therapy) over identification processes. I consider growth through "identification with" a transitory process while self-actualization through "differentiation from" is a lifelong mode of self-assertive living.

Fay B. Karpf and Maurice J. Karpf expressed their views on interventions in the following statement:

In the consideration of interventions in psychotherapy, whether the concern is directly with values or less directly with choices and decisions more generally, it seems necessary from our standpoint to differentiate between therapy cases and counseling cases even though they so frequently overlap.

Insofar as therapy cases are concerned, we believe that the patient is, in the first place, entitled to information relative to his problems, which he may lack and which may not

---

3. An exception to this point of view and the rationale for the exception is quoted from Dr. Simkin on pp. 205 ff.

be easy to come by in our highly specialized culture. The therapist can provide the necessary information if the subject is within his experience and competence, or he can refer the patient to other community resources. Once such information is at hand and is adequately considered in therapy in terms of possibilities and alternatives, it is then up to the patient to decide upon his course of action within the framework of the therapeutic process. The earnest therapist will no doubt give the patient a push, here and there, in the direction which he considers wise in view of the patient's concrete situation and value perspective, both personal and cultural, but the actual decision is always up to the patient himself. This is not only necessary for therapeutic progress but, more important, for his continuing development.

If the patient is made to feel from the beginning that his problems are *his* and the responsibility for their solution or resolution is his, he will not expect the therapist to assume the responsibility for actually directing his choices and decisions. He will only expect help toward making sound choices and decisions himself, and to such help he is, of course, entitled. As already indicated, this includes necessary information as well as therapeutic preparation.

If the patient is temporarily so confused regarding his goals and values as to be unable, for the time being, to make necessary choices and decisions, it may become necessary to enlist the cooperation of those closest to him (with the patient's permission, of course). In such an event, the therapist of necessity has to be more obtrusively active, but again, not to take on the responsibility for specifically directing the patient's choices and decisions but to secure for him the additional aid that he at the moment may require. From our standpoint, it is important not only to build up the patient himself in such a case but also to surround him with supporting resources in the form of relatives, friends, and community services, that is, his natural supporting environment —to the end always that he may become as soon as possible, within the full range of his potentialities, a self-reliant person.

The weaker he is in personal resources, the more supporting cooperation of this type he will require. But for the therapist to take on this directive responsibility is to provide the patient with a crutch which he will not readily relinquish and which, furthermore, will interfere with his self-development.

The situation may be somewhat different with counseling cases. Here, we deal for the most part with people of a more or less normal self-reliance. We can discuss with them alternatives and consequences much more freely and feel that they for the most part will proceed on their own toward (for them) proper solutions.

If they are emotionally disturbed because of the nature of their problems or the obstacles to their desired solution, they become in varying degrees therapy cases and the procedure correspondingly needs to be modified along the lines already noted for such cases.

Hedda Bolgar made the following statement:

It seems to me that the essential experience of the patient in therapy is the discovery of himself and his growing capacity to trust his own reactions. With the feeling that his impressions, his desires, his decisions are "right," comes the feeling of acceptance by others and with that a mutuality and freedom in all relationships. This can be accomplished only if the therapist consistently avoids supplying solutions no matter how subtly or with how much verbalized insistence that the patient make his own choices. Only by exploring over and over the patient's need to be guided by the therapist's solutions (and incidentally, also by exploring the therapist's need to guide) can we help the patient overcome the feeling of his own worthlessness and his need to live somebody else's life rather than his own. I realize that my emphasis on the patient's autonomy represents part of my own value system and that, in a sense I cannot help but convey this to my patients. But hopefully, all I do convey is a basic attitude. Even if the patient chooses to adopt the same attitude, through imitation or identification, in the working through of its application to his own life problems

24

he will have many opportunities to explore the degree of autonomy in his original choice. Needless to say, this is a statement of my theoretical position; in practice, I am sure, I cannot resist the temptation to accept at face value and with an inner glow of satisfaction, the patient's growing in the direction of my own values and I am sure, like most other therapists, I neglect to explore with the patient those experiences and feelings which are therapist-syntonic. I must accept this as my limitation as a human being. But a limitation it is.

The author, on the other hand, declared herself in favor of informative as well as value statements at certain specific occasions. Her rationale is that we live in a time of tremendously fluctuating values with a tremendous, ever-increasing impact of rapid scientific advances on man's interpretation of life's meaning and purpose. This is why, as Allen Wheelis (1958) states, patients apply to the analyst for values that analysis cannot provide (p. 188).

True, the analyst cannot provide them. But he can on occasion, briefly survey for the patient the trends of our time. He can structure for the patient the changes in value orientation and *Weltanschauung* that are taking place and can advise him regarding different possible solutions among which he might choose.

The opinion that everybody should evaluate for himself what he wants to believe in, no matter how complicated the whole issue between science and religion has become, reminds me a little of Jean Jacques Rousseau's postulate that every child should make for himself all the discoveries that science had made up to the eighteenth century. I should think the limitations of the valiant "do it yourself" slogan must be as evident as its advantages.

While I feel that in our time the *structuring of trends in*

25

value orientations should be included among the responsibilities of the therapist, I emphasize on the other hand that the *technique* by which the intervention is accomplished as well as the *timing* of this intervention are of the essence. Furthermore, I want to point out that informative structuring need not necessarily be followed by the therapist's taking a stand. This would seem to be optional; it depends on the patient's personality, the type of case, and the therapist's personality.

If, for example, in the case of the student who feels he should make A's, different philosophies of life relevant to the problem of whether or not one should excel in work had been discussed at the beginning, when the patient still lived in a neurotic dependency relationship with his father, such information would have been useless, and the patient's transference relationship might have been detrimentally affected by the therapist's taking a stand. Only after the patient was freed from the impact of his father would he be able to utilize an objective dicussion of value orientation.

Whether beyond the help in structuring situations with respect to value trends of our time, the patient will also gain from learning the therapist's own philosophy will vary from case to case. However, some therapists do not seem to qualify the occasions for which they recommend this procedure. Thorne (1950) for example includes as a general practice the teaching of a philosophy of life among his counseling methods. Gardner Murphy (1955) feels that the young need help and advice from those who have thought things through.

This, I would definitely qualify. Apart from the fact that many patients' cultural and religious background have given them a frame of reference that leads them to a philosophy of life different from their therapist's, there are also those who are perfectly capable of finding their own stand, after the situation has been structured for them.

Therefore, the occasions in which information and value statements are permissible or desirable, and the manner in which such statements should be made, should be established by research, and examples should be published.

The following study is meant to be a first step in the direction of a more systematic clarification of the whole problem area of values in psychotherapy.

In the current training of psychotherapists a great deal of emphasis is laid on the therapist's self-awareness. He is taught a systematic procedure. The adequacy of the single intervention is a subject of study; there is also an increasing literature on interview techniques. Yet it seems that in spite of studies and supervision, the handling of values is still an open problem. Furthermore, it seems, judging from the findings in the previously referred to study of psychoanalysts and psychotherapists under observation, by Bolgar (In prep.), that much happens that eludes the self-awareness of the therapist.

Among other questions raised, the present study concerns itself with, *Is it possible to formulate some alternative solutions for the handling of value problems in psychotherapy?*

In order to design studies needed to better understand the whole subject of values in psychotherapy, the author (1959b) tried first of all to formulate some general principles that most modern psychotherapists seem to have in common. Briefly named, these principles are: (1) Present-day psychotherapists strive to help the patient to a better understanding of himself in order to help him to *face and accept reality* as it is and to *master his own life* better than he did before; (2) Most modern psychotherapists want the patient

27

to work through his problems by himself as much as possible, with the therapist being mostly an intermediary in the process of self-understanding, rather than a teacher or a knowing authority; (3) The present-day therapists base their work mostly on their *personal relationship* with the patient and on the *interpretations* that they give to the patient's motives, development, affects, and behavior; (4) The therapist's training, experience, and personality that determine this procedure may vary greatly. But regardless of their theoretical bias and their therapeutic approach, they will have to help the patients to cope with their lives, with the goal of *functioning better than before*, of *mastering their lives*, and of conceiving of *life as worthwhile*.

Rudolf Ekstein (1958), in discussing the elements common to all psychotherapy regardless of school, emphasizes that many schools are successful because they all help the patient to *"think things through"* [italics supplied].

Thinking things through and consideration of the worthwhileness of life brings problems of values into focus. All through therapy, value problems and value conflicts come up for discussion, for re-evaluation, for new solutions. Consequently, it seems of prime importance to discuss some of the main existing *concepts of value* and to arrive at some generally acceptable definition, if possible. This may be followed by a discussion and examples of value problems and value conflicts that we encounter in psychotherapy.

28

1 Theoretical Concepts of Values

1.
Definitions of the Concept of Value

The great present-day interest in values has called forth a vast amount of literature on the subject. One of the most comprehensive and systematic studies was published under the editorship of Talcott Parsons and Edward A. Shils (1952), and conducted by a group that met at Harvard University. The study is called *Toward a General Theory of Action* and devotes a large section to the problem of values and value orientation. This comprehensive study seems to offer a good point of departure for our conceptual clarification.

In the Harvard study, values are referred to exclusively as "moral" preferences. Kluckhohn, one of the main contributors writing on the theoretical framework of values, says explicitly: "A value is not just a preference but is a preference which is felt and/or considered to be justified—

29

'morally' or by reasoning or by aesthetic judgments, usually by two or all three of these" (Parsons and Shils, p. 396). In continuing, he emphasizes further that even if only implicitly stated, there is always a reference to the desirable, not only the desired.

This then is a definite difference of point of view from the later inclusion of "factual" values, which we adopt from Margenau (1959).

Kluckhohn's point of view is clearly expressed in a definition he gives as an alternative to several others: "Value may be defined as that aspect of motivation which is referable to standards, personal or cultural, that do not arise solely out of immediate tensions or immediate situations" (Parsons and Shils, p. 425).

This is in agreement with Parsons' and Shils' point of view, when they say: "Patterns of value orientation have been singled out as the most crucial cultural elements in the organization of systems of action" (p. 159). It is also in agreement with Edward Tolman, who states: "Cultures have value standards—cognitive, appreciative, moral." He goes on to say that these standards are "acquired by the actors living in these cultures."

Kluckhohn introduces the concept of value orientation. He says: "It is convenient to use the term value-orientation for those value notions which are (a) general, (b) organized, and (c) include definitely existential judgments. A value-orientation is a set of linked propositions embracing both value and existential elements" (p. 409).

These value orientations symbolize the fact that, "affective-cognitive (value) and strictly cognitive (orientation) elements are blended. More formally, a value-orientation

30

may be defined as a generalized and organized conception, influencing behavior, of nature, of man's place in it, of man's relation to man, and of the desirable and nondesirable as they may relate to man-environment and interhuman relations" (p. 411).

Kluckhohn tries to organize and to classify value orientations in terms of dimensions. There are the dimensions of modality, comprising aesthetic, cognitive, and moral values; intent, comprising instrumental and goal values; generality; intensity; explicitness; extent, in which universal versus personal and group values are discussed; and finally, organization, in which the hierarchy of values and isolated and integrated values are noted.

Although these are all very important distinctions, our own problems of values in psychotherapy calls for some other considerations. Of prime importance in connection with clinical problems is the discussion of values in relationship to needs and goals.

Kluckhohn's discussion of the relationship of values to needs and goals is fairly brief. He summarizes his survey of the literature on the subject of values and needs with the conclusion that "the relationship between a value system and a need or goal system is necessarily complex. Values both rise from and create needs. A value serves several needs partially, inhibits others partially, half meets and half blocks still others."

Values are not identical with *goals*. Kluckhohn agrees with a statement of the Cornell study of values: "Values are not the concrete goals of behavior, but rather are aspects of these goals. Values appear as the criteria against which goals are chosen, and as the implications which these goals have in the situation" (p. 429).

31

This statement of the Cornell group would not prohibit the inclusion of factual preferences under the concept of values nor would it necessitate the limitation of the concept of values to the area of normative preferences.

For the conceptualization and organization of clinical data an all-inclusive value concept seems preferable. In the fluctuating value system of our Western society the theoretically sharp demarcation line between factual and normative values has become problematic, and previously acknowledged standards and norms of behavior have been changed by consensus or have become matters of doubt and debate.

Specifically the area of "consensus" that Parsons and Shils call an "area of permissiveness" is at present in flux. This area of consensus or permissiveness seems to me to represent an area of transition between factual preferences and normative standards. This will be illustrated in further discussions (see pp. 45 ff.).

Suffice it to say that for the clinical understanding of the individual's motivation an all-inclusive value concept as developed by another group seems more commensurate with this specific material. We are referring to the group whose conference results were published in *New Knowledge in Human Values* (1959). This group, under the leadership of A. H. Maslow, was sponsored by the Research Society for Creative Altruism. I will, in working out my definition, adopt a number of considerations that were made by participants in this conference.

First of all, we follow Henry Margenau (1959) who, while distinguishing between factual and normative values, includes both in his value concept. He defines "factual values" as "observable preferences, appraisals, and desires of concrete people at a given time" (p. 39 and "normative

32

values" as ratings "which people *ought* to give to value objects" (p. 39). Margenau finds that this disitinction is widely recognized in philosophic writings. He also points out that normative value is much more difficult to establish than factual value, while, at the same time, it "makes a profounder claim of validity, presumes to have suasive force and regulative power" (p. 39).

In elaborating these two concepts, Margenau expresses the belief that it is fallacious to search for as objective a basis of normative values as exists for factual values. Factual values, he says, have a "fixed abode." They can be discovered in stated preferences, opinion polls, and the like. Factual unconscious preferences, we may add, can be disclosed in depth studies and psychotherapeutic explorations.

Normative values, however, according to Margenau, are searched for in vain in a "static abode in human thought," with "a fixed basis in logic, an a priori origin." In his opinion they are likewise arbitrary as long as they stand by themselves. "Honesty, veracity, friendship, love of mankind, and all the rest: they point to and receive their value from a *command* or *directive* to which a person is *committed*" (p. 42).

This commitment, which may have its basis in either personal or cultural standards, represents perhaps the main difference between factual and normative values.

Bertalanffy (1959) speaks of factual values as in the last analysis *biological* values, while normative values are essentially *symbolic*; they are set up by conscious thinking and develop with progressive cerebralization.

The directive of factual preferences and the directive of norms are both open to *choice*, which in turn is the result of *freedom*. This freedom undoubtedly varies considerably

33

on different levels of development and on different organizational levels of the individual personality and the cultural matrix in which he participates.

Maslow and Fromm have tried to find a valid criterion for standards of evaluating behavior. In the discussion of the conference that was our point of departure, they both take the stand that there are "good choosers" and "bad choosers." Fromm (1959) states that "all answers that can be qualified as 'good' have in common that they are consistent with the very nature of life which is continuous birth and growth" (p. 162). This of course is in itself a value judgment. The same is true of Goldstein's emphasis on health as a value. It is the value concept that seems most natural to our time and culture that Maslow calls the choices of self-actualizing persons that is, a "naturalistic value system." But there are evidently other cultural orientations in which health and life do not have supremacy among values. As early as the twenties Heinz Hartmann (1928), Victor Frankl (1928), and others pointed out the probable lack of validity of the assumption that health was as supreme a value for most people as it seems to be for the therapist.

Most therapists feel committed to restoring their patient's health; they find considerable problems when, with some of their patients, they encounter religious or ethical beliefs that run contrary to the assumption of health as the supreme value. This problem will be further discussed and illustrated in the last sections of this chapter.

If we cannot accept that the value of health or of self-realization is proven to be supreme, is then the relativism that Margenau proclaims the only realistic outlook on the problem of normative values?

We are in the dilemma that, while not knowing any

34

longer what to believe in, mankind feels forever compelled to believe in something. Or at least this is true of the vast majority of people at all times. If recently certain groups, like the existentialists and other thinkers, have pointed out that it is not necessary to believe in anything, this is so far only representative of small intellectual groups. But it must be admitted that the inner necessity with which peoples the world over orient themselves to beliefs and turn to beliefs is obviously their only evidence for the existence of something to believe in. They seem to project their necessity into the universe and people of all times can never be convinced that there is not something in the objective reality of the universe to which they are related or obligated or by which they are determined.

We seem to set up these beliefs as something which we hold on to and they become something that holds us up.

The question is whether there is anything more we can claim about them than that they represent mankind's internal necessity.

2.

Values and Beliefs

Is all we can say about normative values that they are mankind's beliefs that represent a great variety of ideas and that seem to be in constant flux, changing through the times and from one culture to the other?

It seems to me that there might be one other common denominator to these beliefs. They all seem to have what I propose to call a "constructive intent."

The use of the word "constructive," as proposed in the

term "constructive intent" is not related to George A. Kelly's (1955) concept of "construct." Kelly gives the name "construct" to the "ways of construing the world," to the systems that man designed to "fit realms of fact." Construct is, in this sense, an intellectual procedure. It is a method of thinking, by means of which man tries to anticipate what might happen in the future. A "construct" is actually a hypothesis about the future.

The anticipation of the future is also essential for the constructive intent. It, too, operates with the future. But different from Kelly's construct, the constructive intent is an active directedness toward the accomplishing of the most beneficial future; beneficial in whatever sense the persons engaged in the process may understand.

In other words, constructive intent is not a new term like Kelly's construct, but a somewhat more specific application of a popular word. The usage is the same as Carl Rogers' when he speaks of the release of the "constructive tendency" in the patient.

By that I mean, regardless of whether beliefs are actually constructive—sometimes they are quite destructive—beliefs are always set up with the intent of effecting something, that is, upbuilding that which is meant by "good" or upholding that which is meant by "true."

In looking for reasons for these constructive intents represented by the values we believe in, we might think of something like the "metaphysical need" that the existentialist Victor E. Frankl (1956) talks about, "to give account of the purpose of our existence" (p. 82). He says that we feel we have to live up to something and that we feel responsibility for what we do.

Frankl (1957b) assigns to the psychotherapist the tasks

36

of appealing to man's will to meaning and of interpreting this will to meaning in terms of a sense of responsibility. He identifies being conscious and being responsible with being human.

But responsibility to whom? To our own conscience? The question is whether this responsibility functions properly and/or whether its functions have validity. Adolf Eichmann asserted recently in all seriousness that doing his butcher's work was nothing but fulfilling his responsibility. Erikson (1958) brilliantly compares Martin Luther's and Adolf Hitler's convictions regarding their missions in the world. Both were based on what he calls "negative identity." He suggests that "in malignant cases this soon exhausts social resources" (p. 102). But unfortunately Hitler's social resources were quite considerable for a long time.

Frankl's appeal to the patient's sense of responsibility represents the transmittance of a very specific belief. Objections to the teaching of such specific beliefs were raised by several members of the previously mentioned Value Study Group. Dr. Zoltan Gross gave his objections the following formulation:

> Beliefs frequently are premature leaps bridging the chasms that exist in our knowledge of ourselves and the world in which we live. Man's enormous appetite for meaning leads him to indulge in phantasied bouquets of belief. Unfortunately, the nourishment from such indulgences is proportionate only to the congruence between that which is believed and that which exists.
>
> Any fundamental definition of meaning should await clearer understanding of the structural basis of psychological functioning. *These structural formulations must be outside of motivational speculations.* Recent experiments on sensory deprivation provide a glimpse at the underlying psychological machinery that moves the "motives" that direct behavior.

But then what do we do with our patients? Erikson, in discussing our ways of coping with the "metaphysical riddle of existence" comes to the conclusion that the way to accept the limitations of human knowledge and power is to ornament the inevitable with:

> . . . some special pride—pride in our power to resign ourselves, or pride in the inevitable as something so patently good that we surely would have chosen it if it had not chosen us. If adult man, then, ever comes close to an ego-chill, he has available automatic recourse to a *context in which he is needed, or in which others will him so that he may will them, or in which he has mastered some technique which brings visible returns* [italics supplied]. He forgets the sacrifices which he has to make to achieve this functional relatedness to other occupants of his cultural universe. He forgets that he achieved the capacity for faith by learning to overcome feelings of utter abandonment and mistrust; the sense of free will by resigning himself to a mutual limitation of wills; relative peace of conscience by submitting to, and even incorporating into himself, some harsh self-judgments; the enjoyment of reason by forgetting how many things he wanted to solve and could not; and the satisfaction of duty by accepting a limited position and its obligations in his technology (p. 112).

But is this then the whole answer to Crane Brinton's (1953) observation which Erikson quotes:

> To be provocative I shall say all normal people are metaphysicians; all have some desire to locate themselves in a "system," a "universe," a "process" transcending at least the immediate give-and-take between the individual and his environment; for all normal people the conscious lack or frustration of some such understanding will result in a kind of metaphysical anxiety (p. 110).

In V. E. Frankl's terminology man cannot live in an "existential vacuum."

Some people reason that our psychological make-up is such that to be able to act, we need beliefs. This is Julian Huxley's argument, when he says: "We must believe something, for otherwise we should never act. On the other hand, we must not believe everything, or believe too readily, or we shall act wrongly" (p. 14). "When we cannot be certain, we must proceed in part by faith—faith not only in the validity of our own capacity of making judgments, but also in the existence of certain factual realities, pre-eminently moral and spiritual realities" (p. 16).

It may be, of course, that the constructiveness of mankind's intent has actually a *practical basis*. It might, for example, have to do with a long-range foresight of the ultimate benefit derived from the belief in and adherence to these values. George Lundberg in a similar vein ties value judgments to "expectations" (1948, pp. 392 f.).

If, for example, in most cultures "honesty" is considered to be a positive value, while in some other cultures the ability to lie is regarded highly, both cultures hold different convictions about what might be a more beneficial directive.

Heinz Hartmann (1960) is of the opinion that there are common trends in the evolutional history of mankind. He refers to Freud's conviction that the development of civilization shows the trend of growing internalization of aggression in the formation of the superego and to his own conviction that there is a trend to growing ego autonomy in the ways moral codes are formed. This would indicate a development of responsibility with practical constructive intents and benefits.

But the benefits to be derived from the values we set up belong to different spheres of our existence, and hence conflicts between these values seem unavoidable. Mankind has

39

not yet found the formulas that make it possible to take care of the needs of oneself, one's kin, one's group, and one's nation with a simultaneous consideration of others or of mankind as a whole. Many recent writers have referred to these unresolved predicaments of our present beliefs. Rollo May (1953), for example, points to the unresolved conflict between "the individual's right to pursue his own interests" and "such precepts as love thy neighbor, serve the community" as derived from the "Hebrew-Christian tradition allied with ethical humanism" (p. 50).

Many people of our time and civilization find serious value conflicts arising out of the previously mentioned contradiction between health and self-realization as positive values, and the restrictions and rules that certain religious dogmas or conservative family traditions insist upon regardless of individual needs.

The conflicting norms that we find within our present civilization force every individual to make his own decisions. Many different value systems seem to prevail, and all we can see as their common denominator is what we call their constructive intent. The problem of its foundations will be further discussed within the context of the role of values in human life.

3.
About Intrinsic Values

A further important dimension of the value concept is its attribute of being an intrinsic or extrinsic value. Robert S. Hartman (1959) distinguishes three categories of value: *systemic, extrinsic,* and *intrinsic.* Two examples he gives are:

"I value myself systemically if I pretend I am what I would like to be, extrinsically in my social role, intrinsically in being what I am. God is valued systemically in theology, extrinsically in comparative religion, intrinsically in the mystic experience" (p. 26).

He calls the systemic value a "synthetic concept," the extrinsic value an "analytic concept," and the intrinsic value a "singular concept."

I would prefer to use the concept of the "intrinsic" value in terms of an attribute that participates in constituting an object.

It is intrinsic, meaning a constitutive attribute of life processes, to have direction. Goal preference or choice—that is, factual valuing—is a constitutive attribute of any human existence that is more than vegetation but which has developed freedom. In children's development, this ability to choose, incidentally, begins at about ten to twelve months.

While there may be agreement on the thesis that value is intrinsic to human existence, different answers will probably be given to the question of whether or not certain specific values are constitutive attributes of the individual's existence. In other words: are certain values intrinsic to the individual's existence?

To answer this question it is, in my opinion, important to distinguish between factual and normative values.

4.

*Factual and Normative Values as
Related to Intrinsic Values*

Factual values, that is, factual preferences, are intrinsic to the degree to which they are chosen in accordance with an individual's personality requirements. Normative values, on the other hand, are obviously more culturally than individually determined. To what degree a specific normative value happens to represent something that is intrinsic to an individual's own tendencies is quite difficult to establish.

For example, if we first think of the factual values of an individual, we might point to certain likes and dislikes, such as the preference for, or rejection of, certain foods, or certain activities such as doing things with one's hands; or certain interests such as listening to music; or certain inclinations regarding more general conditions of life such as the frequent enjoyment of being among people, or the liking of excitement or continuous activity; or to want to feel useful, accepted, needed; or to please people; and so forth.

It is evident that some of these factual values have a basis in "natural inclinations,"[2] while others were acquired and learned. It is also evident to the clinician that in many cases natural inclinations have been discouraged and changed before or while they were developing.

A child's natural inclination to do things with his hands may have been discouraged in an environment where no construction material was ever made available, or it may have been turned into destructive tendencies by a hostile, demanding, or exploiting environment. In the same way, a child's natural inclination to like people may have been discouraged or turned into hatred.

Not only in childhood, but also later in life, natural inclinations may become modified due to maturation and/or experiences.

---

2. The degree to which even this concept is problematic will be discussed in the next chapter.

Apart from the discouragement or diversion of natural inclinations, some inclinations are inculcated or frankly taught as preferable to the individual's own tendencies or introduced by educational and other environmental influences as additional goals to pursue.

The individual acquires most of his habits by accepting the process, either willingly, resentfully, or without awareness—from the desire for cleanliness to the desire to read the news or to watch the baseball game on T.V.

If then in psychotherapy we speak of *self-realization* as a goal of life and an ultimate value, some of the more obvious problems are to establish the natural inclinations and potentials of a person, to clarify what neurotic displacements and what artificial constructs made a person digress from his original tendencies, and finally, to come to an evaluation of the desirable hierarchical order of the goals to pursue.

The problems connected with the concept of self-realization have not as yet been systematically discussed. Since the finding of the self and self-realization as a goal are problems of great consequence when it comes to values in psychotherapy we will discuss the "self-realization theory" more fully in the next chapter.

If it is difficult to assess the intrinsic nature of the self and of factual preferences, the problem of assessment becomes still more complicated with respect to normative values. The normative values to which an individual commits himself obviously stem from several contributory sources. Cultural and subcultural influences are undoubtedly most effective. The individual's own thinking and his own inclinations may or may not also be contributory to the system of norms to which he subscribes. His system may be altogether an artifact or it may incorporate the intrinsic values of the individual. The way in which the one is superimposed on the other, or how the amalgamation or integration takes place is as yet not really known to us.

Assume a person has, from her early days, been strongly admonished "to be honest and to tell the truth," in terms of describing situations accurately. Assume this person has none of those inclinations that would form a natural basis to this type of being honest.

For example, she—I am taking a case example—is not particularly interested in facts and how things actually are. She pays more attention to her feelings about things. Furthermore, she tends to be dependent, wants to be liked and accepted, and wants to please people rather than stand up to them. This woman frequently will be inaccurate in her statements and will color situations in order to please people, yet she gets highly indignant when anybody intimates that she might not always be sticking to things as they are, because she is deeply convinced of the absolute values of honesty and of her extreme honesty.

The present state of our knowledge is largely that of information obtained from psychoanalytically oriented studies on ego and superego goals. How far intrinsic values—in the sense in which we defined them—are incorporated in ego and superego goal setting is for the present largely a matter of speculation. Yet the genuineness of a person's aspirations and the development toward self-realization depend to a great extent on the person's ability to clarify for himself what his own primary tendencies are.

It is obvious that within the total framework of a person's attempts to master life, his inclinations and his self-realization can only play a relative role, depending on the forces impinging on his existence. Consequently, it must

44

always remain the individual's problem to see just how and to what degree he can bring his own inclinations into play.

5.

Consensus Values

Factual and normative values are presented by Margenau as two distinct categories. However, it seems to me that there are value situations in which these two categories overlap. I refer to a type of value that to certain groups represents a norm, while for others the belief in this value is only factual evidence of what some people believe in.

An example of this may be the value of "popularity." In the American educational system a child's popularity is considered a social value. While not normative to the degree that "honesty" might be considered a norm, Americans find it on the whole very desirable to be popular.

In Europe, on the other hand, the concept of popularity is practically unknown, and when a European learns about it, it is often with surprise; he takes it as factual evidence of what another culture considers a value.

Many other social, cultural, and particularly, many religious norms are of this kind. They represent normative values to the adherant of a particular religion and only factual values to others. We will call these "consensus values."

Extremely interesting with respect to values having group validity is a recent study of John P. Spiegel (1959). He, Florence R. Kluckhohn, and a number of coworkers studied, under the aspects of transference and countertransference, some thought patterns that determine different subcultural groups' thinking on a subconscious level. The authors adopt for this behavior the term, "behavior without awareness," from J. K. Adams. They characterize some general value orientations regarding human nature and human relationships that may be considered representative of certain subcultural groups. For their study they selected three such groups with which they tested in actual psychotherapy work their assumption that the transference relationship would be affected by these patients' ideology.

Florence Kluckhohn (1953) has presented in a previous study a systematic approach to the problem of "dominant and variant value orientations." She singled out five common human problems that she considered of key importance to these considerations. They are questions referring to "the innate dispositions of man, the relation of man to nature, the significant time dimension, the valued personality type, the dominant modality of the relationship of man to other man" (p. 46).

In her systematic approach she created a very basic frame for the study of certain *Weltanschauung* parameters that are undoubtedly codetermined by valuation. Her variables are shown in Table 1.

Table 1—Human Problems and Type Solutions*

Innate Predispositions	Evil (mutable or immutable)	Neither good nor bad (mutable or immutable)	Good (mutable or immutable)
Man's Relation to Nature	Man subjugated to nature	Man in nature	Man over nature
Time Dimension	Past	Present	Future
Valued Personality Type	Being	Being-in-becoming	Doing
Modality of Relationship	Lineal	Collateral	Individualistic

* From F. Kluckhohn (1953, p. 346).

Florence Kluckhohn sees these briefly indicated different viewpoints as related to different subcultures within our present-day American situation.

In a historical perspective, some of these variables sometimes appear related to different periods of one and the same culture. There is, for example, in Western civilization, the striking change to a predominant ideal of "action" from previous centuries' belief in the supremacy of "contemplation," as Hannah Arendt (1959) has recently pointed out.

Within our own present cultural value system, not only do there coexist variant value orientations, but there are constant changes and fluctuations. These disturbing changes and fluctuations apply perhaps less to such basic concepts of our ideology as Florence Kluckhohn has in mind and more to principles that determine directly or indirectly our daily life and daily decisions. The basis of these principles may be confused or may be debatable. Religious, moral, or health and welfare considerations valid to one and invalid to another group, are brought into play and cause serious conflicts for many people. Examples within our daily experience are divorce, extramarital intercourse, birth control, abortions, and so on.

Then there are values that have changed in the course of cultural history, for example, the treatment of minority groups, the treatment of the underprivileged, whether or not the individual has a right to freedom and to the free expression of his opinion, principles of authority in government and family life, indebtedness to parents, and many other principles that have changed or are fluctuating.

The values of this middle area may belong to convictions agreed upon by *consensus of opinion* or may have been set up in terms of doctrines, and it is their fluctuation and/or

47

relative validity that often causes people problems. Parsons
& Shils (1952) point out that consensus represents an "area
of permissiveness" as compared with society's standards and
norms. But in comparison with the individual's freedom of
choice, both consensus and doctrines represent areas of
pressure.

Figure 1—Schematic Presentation of Types of Values.

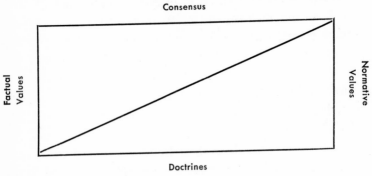

I propose to depict the relationship of these concepts
schematically in a diagram (Figure 1). Factual values and
normative values are at the two opposite ends of the rec-
tangle, while consensus and doctrines are presented on a slid-
ing scale between them. The hypothesis underlying this diagram is then that consensus grows out of a group's factual
values. The more it is developed into doctrines, the closer it
comes to norms.

For example, if in a certain community, first individuals
and then ever-increasing groups feel that all people should
have equal rights, there may be increasing consensus about
this fundamental principle of democracy. As consensus in-
creases, the conviction may become a doctrine that might be

taught, and eventually a norm that might be legalized and enforced. The process is one of increasing pressure and enforcement. (This example does not necessarily depict the actual historical process.)

An opposite process might be exemplified by the lessening rigor of marital laws. The ethical norm and legal enforcement of the permanence of marital vows having been abandoned, and divorce having been legalized, there may still be doctrines about the sacrament of matrimony kept in force by certain religious or lay institutions; then there may be consensus for or against divorce in certain groups. Finally, individuals may have personal convictions regarding the factual values of the permanence or the liquidation of marriages.

2 Values, the Self, and Personality Theory

1.
Values and Needs

The relationship between values and needs is seen very differently from the standpoint of various personality theories.

To Gardner Murphy (1947), an example of one point of view, this relationship does not appear problematic. He says, "the central fact about values [is] that they arise from definite wants" (p. 272). These wants all are of types but ultimately they "can never reach beyond the tissue needs from which they originally spring. The tissues themselves, however, have changed as the drive developed, so that it is a different individual who now wants the Bach music or the Masefield poem" (p. 272).

In a way this is opposite to Clyde Kluckhohn's point of

50

view. He, as we saw in the last chapter, considers the relationship between a value system and a need system to be very complex and not necessarily compatible. "A value," he says, "serves several needs partially, inhibits others partially, half meets and half blocks still others." In other words, Kluckhohn points out that a value may be recognized as such, but not be wanted in any sense.

The conflict between values that serve needs and those that represent need antagonistic–norms is of course one of the major concerns of the psychotherapist. The psychoanalytic theory of the conflict between id and superego gives a model for the understanding and handling of this conflict, as does the eventual internalization of the superego's demands, which then become "needs." But the problem of values has become further complicated by the realization that there is a third aspect to be considered besides that of needs and norms belonging neither to the category of needs nor of norms. These are those cultural values of whose variety and relativity modern cultural anthropology has made us aware.

2.
The Problem of Cultural Values and Psychoanalysis

Only recently has it been increasingly realized that certain directions that an individual receives from his sociocultural environment are not of the same order as the directions derived from his personal needs or from his moral code. In fact, it is this increasing recognition of the fluctuation of our own Western social and cultural values that has brought the value problem to the fore.

Previously, the psychoanalytic teaching was that the

superego became representative of a universally operative human society's demands as transmitted by the parents.

"In Freud's investigations," says George J. Mohr in his article, "Psychoanalysis: Some Present-Day Assessments" (1960), "the qualitative uniqueness of the individual emerged against a background of psychological dynamisms presumably universally operative, regardless of the particularities of social or cultural environment. During the past quarter century, a frame of reference in which it is assumed that the individual can be understood only as a member of a social group has been utilized" (p. 16).

The separation of the two categories of moral and of sociocultural values calls for a modification of the psychoanalytic theory on which certain psychoanalysts are working. The volume *Psychoanalysis and Human Values*, edited by Masserman, is largely devoted to this problem.

Helen V. McLean for example presents it this way:

> There is in the psychoanalytic literature a tendency to equate values with morals, or to confuse ego attitudes which are called values with admonitions and injunctions arising from the superego. Ego values may be consonant with the moral commands of the superego, but values may also be opposed to the archaic, rigid demands of the superego.
>
> The problem of values is a problem of ego psychology. Both the unconscious and conscious ego mediates on the one hand between inner needs, id impulses, shall we say, and the superego or moral faculties—and on the other hand, the demands of the culture (p. 104).

The kind of impact these demands of culture represent is seen in a different light by different authors. Fritz Redlich (1960) for example considers it of such consequence that he even feels that different cultures call for completely different therapeutic approaches.

52

Heinz Hartmann (1960) on the other hand feels that there is a "relativism" "that tends to underrate the common elements shared by different moral systems" (p. 82). He believes there are common trends in the evolutional history of mankind. He takes one example from Freud: "For him the growing internalization of aggression in the formation of the superego was a main trend in the development of civilization." Another is his own: "A trend toward growing ego autonomy, which we believe to be manifest in the development of at least some civilizations, may play a role, too, in the ways moral codes are formed" (p. 84).

The prevailing tendency seems to be to realize that the diversity of cultural directives becomes an increasingly confusing factor. One of the reasons is that our own cultural tradition seems to us increasingly more problematic (see pp. 35 ff.). Another reason is that with the intensified communications and exchanges that take place from one culture to another, we are daily more aware of many possible and perhaps equally valid attempts to tackle the problems of human life.

A theoretical question is how those cultural values that are not explicitly transmitted by authorities come to the individual. From the psychoanalytic point of view, the main vehicle of transmission would probably be the process of *identification*, although strangely enough this important concept is not treated in Masserman's volume.

The capacity for and process of identification are generally thought to develop in the wake of incorporation and introjection. As described by Rapaport (1951) the drive-cathecting of memory-traces of previous drive-objects is the process of introjecting.

Introjected objects constitute major suborganizations within the developing memory-organizations of the ego—that is the superorganization of drive-controls—which grows on the renunciation of drive-objects necessitated by the environment, maturation and development. These organizations which arise in the ego in the wake of an introjection are conceptualized as *identifications*. Indeed, from certain vantage points, the ego is the precipitate of abandoned drive-objects, that is, of identifications (Freud). On the one hand, these introjected objects become integrated, lose their independence, and give rise to a homogeneous ego, whose strength is greatly dependent on the completeness of their integration; on the other hand, they give rise to the ego-ideal and the superego, which permit the individual to see himself with the eyes of others, and thus to make himself and his thoughts the object of his observation. Introjection and identification thus enable us to take over, as our own, the feelings and reactions of other people, and later their thoughts also—both those directed specifically towards us and those more general (pp. 724-725).

The complexity of the process of identification is acknowledged by many. R. R. Grinker (1957) critically surveys different theoretical assumptions about it. The most important seems to me to be Grinker's succinct distinction between the "ego" and the "self." In discriminating his ideas from several of the previously named authors who assign the social role development to the ego, Grinker says: "I believe that we have conceptually fused ego functions, which are a part of personality, with all of personality as a boundary process capable of integrating and organizing, and maintaining psychological homeostasis. We should allocate such functions to the 'self,' a supra-ordinate structure capable of integrating the many subsystems, including the many identifications that constitute the ego, and of organizing

54

behavior into available social roles. Much of psychodynamics can be better understood if we appreciate the differences between ego and 'self' " (p. 27).

The self is, in Grinker's thinking a superstructure, a *resultant* "composed of many identifications" (p. 13). The difference between the psychoanalytic resultant self and the self-realizationists' self, which seems to be thought of as underlying rather than as resultant, will be discussed later.

A somewhat intermediate position is taken by Erikson, in that "identity" covers all the characteristics of the individual, while "self" refers only to the core. Erikson has devoted some of the most comprehensive studies to the problem of identity, as well as to that of the social and cultural roles developed by means of identification. In pointing out the various attributes of identity, he seems still to struggle with the clarification of this complex concept.

In his latest publication (1959), he distinguishes *personal identity* as based on "the immediate perception of one's selfsameness and continuity in time; and the simultaneous perception of the fact that others recognize one's sameness and continuity," and *ego identity*, which, "concerns more than the mere fact of existence, as conveyed by personal identity; it is the ego quality of this existence" (p. 23). At a later place in the same book, Erikson speaks, however, of a "conscious sense of *individual identity*," and also of an "unconscious striving for a continuity of personal character." He mentions further an "ego synthesis," an "inner solidarity with a group's ideals and identity" and a "world wide public identity." He also speaks of "cultural identity."

Erikson describes the complex genesis of the process of identity formation, which "emerges as an evolving configuration—a configuration which is gradually established by successive ego syntheses and resyntheses throughout childhood; it is a configuration gradually integrating constitutional givens, idiosyncratic libidinal needs, favored capacities, significant identifications, effective defenses, successful sublimations, and consistent roles" (p. 116).

Erikson feels that there is a preconscious aspect to conscious identity. He sees it in a preconscious "sense of psychosocial well-being" (p. 118). This observation refers, however, only to one aspect of identity, that is the aspect of *inner assuredness*.

As far as the roots of identity are concerned, Erikson sees them actually in what he calls *"inner sameness and continuity."* This represents another aspect than those of assuredness and identification. This sameness is manifested, says Erikson, in congenital behavior attributes. It is manifested in those not yet definable subtle singular characteristics of a person's movements, manners, and style.

The moment we talk about "inner sameness and continuity," about "constitutional givens," about "congenital behavior attributes," we refer of course to something completely different from a "superstructure" and a "resultant." Now we refer to something underlying, something primary, which to fit into the psychoanalytic system would require a rather radical change of the original ego and reality concept. It would require the assumption of a basically positive reality, because this underlying, primary something, this basic person, if there is such a thing, moves into reality with a "trust" (Erikson), or rather a capacity for trust. I myself would not consider it as only reactive, but as basic. The "curious" and "interested" infant moves around with "anticipations determined by positive aspects of reality" (C. Buhler, 1954).

While a development in psychoanalytic theory in this direction seems to be on the way, its systematic position within the whole of psychoanalytic theory is not yet clear.

3.

The Value Concept in the Theory of Self-Realization and in Existentialism

When the self-realization theorists speak of the self, one gets the impression that they mean something really underlying, some core. Their "potentialities" sound like something substantial, something there in the bud, so to speak, beginning with conception. The question is what exactly do or can they mean?

C. S. Hall and Lindzey (1957) in their survey of personality theories, in which they deal extensively with the self-actualization theory of Goldstein and Maslow, and with Rogers' Self-theory make a point of emphasizing that in the Self-theories the self is "a name for a group of processes" (p. 468). It "is not an homunculus or a 'man within the breast' or a soul" (p. 468).

Well, it may not be an homunculus, but if it is something that "strives for consistency," that experiences itself as a "center" (Rogers), it must to my mind be thought of as a "structure," a dynamic structure to be sure, but not just "a group of processes."

Hall and Lindzey summarize Rogers' statements about the self under the following points:

The self, which is the nuclear concept in Rogers' theory of personality, has numerous properties some of which are these: (a) it develops out of the organism's interaction with the environment, (b) it may introject the values of other

57

people and perceive them in a distorted fashion, (c) the self strives for consistency, (d) the organism behaves in ways that are consistent with the self, (e) experiences that are not consistent with the self-structure are perceived as threats, and (f) the self may change as a result of maturation and learning (p. 478).

While Rogers' self thus seems in some way the core of the growing and striving organized whole, it does not seem identical with that which is valuable. Values seem in Rogers' theory not part of the core, but they "accrue to the self-picture" and "are also taken over from others." "Experiences become invested with values" (p. 483).

Rogers' self seems different from Horney's and Fromm's and from Goldstein's and Maslow's in that these self-realization theorists seem to see value emerge with the unfolding process as such. "Good in humanistic ethics," says Erich Fromm, "is the affirmation of life, the unfolding of man's powers" (1947, p. 20). He goes back to Aristotle's deduction of "the norm that 'virtue' (excellence) is 'activity' by which he means the exercise of the functions and capacities peculiar to man" (p. 25). And Fromm emphasizes that it is "constant vigilance, activity, and effort" which "can keep us from failing in the one task that matters—the full development of our powers within the limitations set by the laws of our existence" (p. 45).

In a similar vein, Karen Horney (1950) thinks of the self as something "innate" and speaks of "the real self as that central inner force common to all human beings and yet unique in each, which is the deep source of growth" (p. 226).

A third representative of this group, Kurt Goldstein (1939) speaks of a "drive" that enables and impels the organism to actualize in further activities, according to its nature (p. 197). Goldstein emphasizes that optimal self-actualization also means health.

Maslow (1959) speaks of a naturalistic "value system" according to which the healthy person makes good choices. Desirability, health, and value are seen as closely related, if not identical.

This self of the self-realization theorists, which is "a central inner force" and which seems to have direction and a creative intent, appears similar to the "creative self" of the later Alfred Adler, as a kind of a nucleus that Hall and Lindzey call "not unlike the older concept of soul" (p. 125).

In contradistinction to the self-realizationist self, the *existential* self is not at all biologically determined, as Binswanger (1944/5) emphasizes. Existence transcends being. The self represents a potential mode of being, chosen by the individual as a result of his ability to transcend his being. In his freedom man "designs" his self as well as his "world"; both being reciprocal concepts.

Although the concept of self-realization is used by some existentialists, it is not used in the same sense as by the self-realization theorists. V. E. Frankl (1960) is particularly emphatic on the point that "man's concern is not to 'fulfill himself' or to 'actualize himself' but to fulfill 'meaning' and to 'realize value'" (p. 3). Gebsattel, too, (1959) speaks of the realization of the 'personal existence' (*personales Dasein*) in the sense of the realization of a task that transcends the individual himself.

In other words, while the self-realization theorist's solution of life is immanent and experienced as the life process itself, the existentialists' solution of life is transcendent and becomes real in the product or result of life.

59

Yet this result is not the same as the psychoanalytic resultant self and value. The difference is that while the existential self is not biologically determined, man's freedom of choice is, after all, still an outcome of his nature and not a product of society or culture. As Binswanger points out in referring to Goldstein's studies, "a defective organism . . . can produce organized behavior only by such limitation of its milieu as corresponds to its defect" (p. 199).

4.

Value in Cultural Anthropology and Social Psychology

If for purposes of visualization we were to draw a line and put at one end "nature," at the other "society and culture" as the sources from which the "self" and "value" originate, then the self-realization theorists would be located at the former, and certain groups of social psychologists and cultural anthropologists at the latter end.

To these latter groups, the human being is at no time determined by his "nature" as such. At all times and from the beginning, the individual's own natural tendencies are being influenced and modified from the outside. Since the beginning of his life, as was first strongly contended by James Baldwin (1913), the infant is in a give-and-take relationship with his environment, he grows in mind by absorbing the other person. In asking himself, is the individual a socialized self or an *individualized social self*. Baldwin answers emphatically that the latter is true.

Fay Karpf (1932) shows the development of this point of view in her book *American Social Psychology*. She shows the development of this theory from Baldwin and his predecessors through Cooley, Ross, Dewey, and Thomas to the early thirties. Ross, for example, expresses these thoughts in terms of the "domination of society over the individual." To Baldwin's theory of imitation as the first vehicle of the individual's transformation into a social self, Ross adds the effect of suggestion.

In her summary Karpf states as the essential doctrine of interaction, which social psychology developed against instinct psychology, that the "springs to human action" are not essentially innate, but "that they are social 'in the germ,' so to speak, in consequence of the fact that they are socially defined, conditioned, and directed and by virtue of the very process of social give-and-take in which they function and come to concrete expression. In the terms suggested by one writer recently, they are social products, not biological data. Or, as the issue has been stated by another writer, human impulses are not first biological and then social; they are 'socio-biologic' from the first" (p. 421).

The point of view is also supported by Sullivan (1947) who has argued against the concept of the individual personality and defines the self in terms of "reflected appraisal," and a similar view transpires from the writings of recent social psychologists such as Marvin Opler (1956).

Opler expresses the modern version of this point of view in a number of statements, two of which may be quoted. One is:

> The necessity of recognizing cultural factors as setting more general and pervasive limitations on human behavior than biological needs which, in humans, never act alone, . . . is of crucial importance in the understanding of both normative or aberrant behavior patterns (p. 113).

61

Still more to the point of the "individualized social self" is the following passage:

A person may give to this life-way or this world view his own interpretation in its affective dimensions, but he can no more create it from the outset than any one individual can design from the whole cloth of personalized abstractions any cultural product. If he can synthesize and integrate ideas, perceptions and emotions at all, he must do so in a manner and with an interpretation culled from experience in a larger more or less systematic patterning of human reactions about him. The regulatory controls, the styles of expression, the ordained goals, and social role of behavior are defined within the definition of the situation (its meanings and communicated symbols) long before anyone of us is privileged to select and construct a life pattern, or indeed, add personal understanding and interpretation to it (p. 195).

This theory of the individualized social self is similar to the psychoanalytic point of view in that it makes society and culture responsible for the individual's value system rather than nature. The differences lie in the fact that this group of social psychologists do not accept Freud's triadic personality concept and consequently do not distinguish between ego and superego types of values; furthermore, they reject of course the separate operation of the biological id factor.

Therapeutically speaking, Otto Rank's method of therapy, which has been succinctly presented by Fay Karpf (1939), seems to be the most closely related to the views of social psychology. Although Rank does not describe the individual as so completely determined by his environment as the above mentioned social psychologists, he on the other hand does not visualize that opposition between the individual and the social world of which Freud conceives. To Rank, the individual needs society for his own harmonious development

62

and self-realization. The latter is an expression of active will and leads to a creative self-expression that is "constructive," in terms of society.

A sort of intermediate position between social psychology, psychoanalysis, and the self-realizationists is taken by Kardiner (1946). For him the specific needs of the human organism are in relative independence from and in reciprocal relationships to codified social patterns. He thinks of the individual's relationship with society in terms of an integration and he feels that value systems cut across all other systems, from basic need or primary systems to secondary institutions. His thinking seems to come close to the position that will be taken later by the author.

The difference between the social psychologists and the thinking that seems suggested by the most recent biological findings—see in the following pages the survey of Eiduson, Eiduson, and Geller (in press)—lies in a very specific point. The problem does not lie in the assumption of a predominance of the psychosocial over the biological factor in human development. I do not necessarily see a difficulty in accepting a statement such as Julian Huxley has made in a recent speech: "Man's evolution is not biological but psychosocial: it operates by the mechanism of cultural tradition, which involves the cumulative self-reproduction and self-variation of mental activities and its products . . . ideological instead of physiological or biological organization." The unclear point, however, in this kind of formulation is where exactly it leaves us with respect to heredity. Preferable to me is the more precise formulation of Waddington (1960), when he states that "in addition to this mechanism of individual hereditary transmission, man has developed another system of passing on information. This is the process of social teaching and learning, and it constitutes in effect a secondary mechanism by which evolution can be brought about." Waddington calls the process "socio-genetic," a term which I find less equivocal than "psychosocial."

For me, the problem lies at the specific point where I have to ask myself: *what at all is left of the individual?* From Opler's statement, it looks as if nothing at all were left, as if the individual must be considered completely directed and formed, actually swallowed up by his environment. Although Opler says, "a person may give to this lifeway or this world his own interpretation in its affective dimensions," this is in a way later negated in his statement, that the individual's synthesis and integration of ideas, perceptions, and emotions take place in patterns that he picks up.

And indeed, the evidence presented by modern sociological and anthropological research seems overwhelming. Opler's brilliant summary is a striking survey of the relationship of environmental factors to pathology; from the role of *life experiences* as already stressed by Adolf Meyer, through that of *social class* and *ethnic group* membership as stressed by Redlich, J. A. Clausen, Georgene Seward, and many others, to that of *cultural patterns*, as investigated by Stainbrook, Berenberg and Jacobson, and others.

Stainbrook (1952) in his discussion of his findings with the South American Bahians distinguishes between *clinical* and *cultural* manifestations. He says: "In brief, clinic is not culture, but cultural phenomena greatly affect the etiology and symptoms of psychopathology" (p. 79).

But then, where is the individual? Because in the clinical manifestation the environment and its pressure system are also documented. *Where precisely does individual choice and*

64

responsibility set in and where does it end? If the individual is so overwhelmingly determined by environmental factors, this seems to take freedom and responsibility completely out of the individual's range. Yet we think of the individual as having the capacity, as well as the responsibility, of *direction* and *choice*. The precise question is just exactly how much choice and direction or freedom and responsibility can mean within the complicated conditions of human development. While I do not believe that as yet we are anywhere near a definite answer to this question, we can, I think, say that there are various situations where one could look for an answer.

For example, as will be shown in the next chapter, the most recent biological and child psychological research support the assumption of an initial *selective reactivity* and *self-directive activity* in the newborn. This means an individual response and activity pattern within the given circumstances. Then we find a little later, at about four to five years of age, the first *self-determinations* to goals and ideals, which in the non-neurotic child seem to evolve out of the individual's own potentialities.

But then, as time goes on, and as ideas and prejudices infiltrate, things become increasingly complicated. How does individuality stand up under the impact of these ideas and prejudices? Which individual can, to what degree and with what motivation, break through these entanglements?

Intrapersonal culture conflicts prevent, under certain circumstances, the establishing of an identity, as shown in several case examples in Georgene Seward's book *Clinical Studies in Culture Conflict.* These individuals were partly unable to make definite choices or to *integrate* the chosen cultural patterns into the whole of a personality. This book marks a beginning of the study of the dynamics of *decisions* made regarding cultural preferences.

5.
Multiple Determinants of Self and Value

Recently, intermediate positions regarding the determinants of self and value have been chosen by an increasing number of analysts. Of note in this connection are Erik Erikson's (1959) studies on "identity" to which we referred before. Erikson feels that while Freud's use of the term identity "points to an individual's link with the unique values, fostered by a unique history of his people," it also points to "something in the individual's core" (p. 102). This identity concept has conscious as well as unconscious aspects.

The same is true of Ginsburg's and Herma's (1953) definition. They believe that "the id as well as the ego and superego participate in the establishment of values" (p. 552), although they consider, like Erikson, that the "ego-character of values" is the most cogent aspect.

The authors of the volume *Psychoanalysis and Human Values* also show a tendency in the direction of a new intermediate position in which the triad personality assumes a new role. In this new development, the dynamic interplay of id, ego, and superego is being revised, with Hartmann's (1939) "autonomous ego" coming to the fore as it emerges from the primitive ego-id matrix and becomes capable of being the basic constituent of a normal, that is, healthy process.

The reason for these developments is that the various extreme positions have increasingly been proven as untenable and therefore abandoned.

66

In attempting to find some stable ground on which to stand while trying to evaluate various positions, we might look first of all into the present status of scientific knowledge.

Scientifically speaking, the present-day picture of the nature-nurture problem is very complex, but the most recent findings eliminate with certainty the usefulness of any of the extreme positions.

According to the more recent research on heredity and environment, these two factors are no longer as clear-cut as they once seemed. In following a comprehensive survey of B. T. Eiduson, S. Eiduson, and Geller (in press), we must first of all recognize that neither growth nor learning are distinguishable simple processes.

> Previously, psychologists were very ready to label as learned those facets of behavior which were separate from central nervous system growth, responsive to experience and manipulation, to change or extinction, characteristics which were distinguished by their variability and mutability, as contrasted to a hereditary mechanism which was more fixed and constant. This whole notion has been shown to be inappropriate in recent years. Sperry, the psychobiologist, tells us that in individual development the central nervous system must be sufficiently complex for coordinating any level of behavior when behavior begins, and this inevitably involves learning. Thus learning is indistinguishable from CNS growth, and is additionally, intraorganismic (p. 10).

If then from the beginning, growth and learning are to be considered not two, but rather one interwoven process, any extreme assumption about the determination of development by either the innate or the environmental factors is eliminated.

Since nothing as yet is known about the relative strength

or determining role of either factor, we are left to speculation with only a few further data to go by.

Any living organism according to Eiduson, *et al.*, starts with a given genetic set-up acting in a given environment"; the individual's central nervous system acts as coordinator of the process; and from the beginning there are individual differences which may be responsible for variability of potentialities and for sensitivity degrees. "In one individual an environmentally produced agent can lead to pathology; while in another, an equivalent syndromy can be caused by genetically induced substances" (Eiduson, Eiduson, Geller, p. 5).

We might speculate that these data speak for *primary activity* and *selectivity* on the individual's side.

On the side of the environment determining development, we might cite that there are definite conditions of time and space that decide whether certain developments take place or not and in which form they occur; furthermore, drastic environmental changes are now proved to have drastic effects on development, even on the intra-uterine level (Thompson and Hockman, 1956).

There is no information available as to the degree to which the individual or his environment determine the actual structuralization that takes place, but since distinctive individual differences have been noted, it is reasonable to assume that in some cases the *genetic*, in other cases the *environmental* factor is the stronger and more predominant.

As far as the *self* is concerned, we might assume that the genetic setup that becomes active and the selectivity of its operations represent something which we might call a "core" or a "rudimentary self."

The conclusions which Bernice T. Eiduson (1958) arrives at herself on the basis of her and her collaborators'

68

extensive and brilliant survey, are similar to ours. She concludes that:

> The brain, unlike a machine into which any mechanism can be set, appears to have mechanisms of its own, which serve not only to effect transmission between organism and environment, but even more directly, to contribute substantially to how, when and what will effect the organism. This is not to be construed as in any way a reification of mind or brain, or any declaration of complete independence for organism apart from environment. It is rather a recognition of certain patternings or autonomous qualities which by the nature of their structure and mechanisms perhaps predetermine to a large extent the stimuli which are appropriate to them (p. 204).

This then is in essence the recognition of the individual himself as the selective and directive primary determiner of his own fate.[1]

Summarizing our conclusions from the available scientific findings, they lead us to the assumption that the individual is the primary codeterminant in an otherwise largely unpredictable interaction process between individual and environment.

If then beyond these limited conclusions, further-reaching hypotheses are formulated, such as the trends to self-actualization and self-realization or the formative patterning from the side of environment and culture, both could be regarded as only two directional facets of an evolutional process that is complex from its onset.

However, both are still meaningful facets, in as much as both, the developmental process as well as the environmental

---

1. Just how much this can mean under individually varying impacts of circumstances and individually varying strength of self-determination will still have to be discussed further.

impact, take effect in definite patterns. The development follows the pattern of growth, reproduction, and decline allowing for a process of self-actualization and self-realization; this can be accepted, if it is understood that we speak of a complex self that is constantly in some degree of flux and far more complex than its original core.

The environment on the other hand provides a definite setting and patterns of behavioral rules into which the individual has to fit himself. This can be accepted if it is understood that the individual reacts selectively and represents an influence on the pattern by virtue of his own activity.

Eiduson *et al.* indicate that the process of interaction between a given genetic setup and a given environment is determined from the beginning by a great number of variables capable of exercising different influences on the actual development. Examples of such variables are sensitivity periods or "critical periods" in which things are likely to happen, certain conditions necessary for the development of particular aptitudes, and the like.

Generally speaking, we might distinguish between *potentiality-increasing* or *potentiality-decreasing* internal and external conditions. We call the first *constructive* or *positive*, the second *destructive* or *negative* determinants. It is obvious that the positive or constructive determinants enhance an *expansive* development of an individual while the negative or destructive determinants are *limiting* to it.

Although with the reference to behavioral observations we are moving to the realm of much less stringent scientific data, there is no reason why parallel considerations could not be applied. This process of potentiality-increasing or -decreasing determinants on the biological level has its parallel on the personality development and behavior level.

The newborn infant displays behaviorally, as our observational studies have shown (C. Buhler and H. Hetzer, 1927), from the onset two types of movement. We have called them "moving toward" or "positive" and "moving away from" or "negative" reactions (pp. 141 ff.). We find the appearance of both from the first day of life on. From the fourth month on, we observe "flight" and "defense" movements as well, that is, more complicated movements, namely movements toward an object with a negative intent.[2]

The stimuli causing these reactions are at the beginning mostly tactile or acoustic. The reactions consist in head turning, general body movements, and crying as well as various reflexes.

Aside from these reactions to definite stimuli, the newborn displays from the beginning a so-called spontaneous mass activity of the body that within a few weeks develops into directed movements toward objects. Grasping and an active looking around belong to the earliest activities of this kind.

Both the reactions and the exploratory active movements show an active interest in the outside world. They give evidence of a primarily positive orientation toward "reality" into which the baby moves with a positive anticipation of good things to be found. Only when this reality appears to be hurtful or overwhelming does the reaction become one of withdrawal or defense.

According to psychoanalytic writings, this type of "positive reality" can only be experienced as long as a function

2. Several years later (1945) Horney developed a theory of neurosis, "whose dynamic center is a basic conflict between the attitudes of 'moving toward,' 'moving against,' and 'moving away from' people" (p. 18). Considering the fundamental nature of these three types of movements which we established in infants from early on, her theory obviously hits some pretty basic facts.

71

is what Hartmann (1939) calls "neutral" or conflict-free. This applies mostly to the realms of perception, memory and motility.

The question is, what would be the *motives* of this type of functioning, what is its aim? Even if purely biological (since primary and yet not libidinal), the activity would have to have a purpose. I see the purpose in an expansive thrust forward toward whatever there is to be creatively active with, while simultaneously adapting to its given qualities. Thus the alternatively stretched out and bent fingers are experimented with and the first grasp of the rattle is tried out, all before three months are over.

The satisfactions at these successful manipulations, which K. Buhler (1929) called "function pleasure" and "pleasure of creative mastery," are considered by him as well as also by me as distinguishable from whatever narcissism and cathectic tendencies there may also be in the picture.

It is only a minor argument that also activities in perception, memory and motility may be frustrated from early on and that there are conflicts between the baby's curiosity and fear in the face of "new" stimuli and situations. Hartmann (1958) himself points this out and admits that the functions of this neutral area do not necessarily "remain untouched by mental conflict" (p. 8). His concept of "intrasystemic conflict" is congenial to the concept of conflicting basic tendencies.

The assumption that the infant moves into the world motivated by the "trust" and expectation to be able to become active in a pleasurable and mastering manner, implies a basic outlook toward *challenge* as a potentially positive experience. In this there seem to be great individual differences. It seems to me that from nearly the beginning of

72

his life, the individual *"interprets"* difficulties as either challenges or else as frustrations. Depending not only on the way he is being handled, but also on his own capacity to overcome the hurt over a failure or refusal and to conquer the difficulty or opposition, the individual infants react quite differently to similar situations.

As is widely acknowledged by many authorities on infant behavior, there are right from the beginning great individual differences in activity degrees, aggressiveness or passivity and sensitivity. Would these differences not apply to both, the handling of the libidinal as well as the world of objects which have to be mastered the same as emotions?

The interpretation of the world as a positive or negative reality is to a great extent determined by the individual's adequacy feelings. A distorted picture of the world as a hostile reality does often include objective circumstances besides people. This picture begins with the hypersensitive child when it is overwhelmed by too loud sounds or other too strong stimuli, and it is not necessarily limited to libidinal disappointments.

We do not yet know much about correlations between reactions to people and to the world of objects.

Some interesting data have become available through the informative studies of Escalona and her collaborators. Escalona and Heider (1959) found, for example, low perceptual and low social sensitivity highly correlated, while the opposite correlation was not quite as marked. They found fearfulness of new surroundings and fearfulness of strangers to be relatively independent phenomena.

In an unpublished Viennese study of Gerda Kautsky we found a seemingly high percentage of eight-month-old babies in which the eagerness to play with a new toy was mutually exclusive with the desire to be picked up and have the examiner occupy herself with the baby.

Weil, Alpert, and Neubauer (1956) conclude on the basis of psychoanalytic work with schizophrenic children that hypo- and hyperaggressive tendencies occur in conjunction with hypo- and hyperlibidinal drive energies.

Escalona and Heider (1959) find that "availability of energy," a factor that included as related variables "activity level, zest, the ability to resist stress, and the capacity to draw upon energy reserves while under stress" was of "central importance for the child's total pattern of growth and adaptation" (p. 241). They feel furthermore that activity level perhaps best reflects an individual's potential (p. 237 f.).

The authors state that their findings "support the hypothesis that both activity level and sensory thresholds in infancy play a predisposing role in the development of some later patterns of psychological functioning" (p. 239).

These elaborate studies confirm to a large extent some of our earliest infant observations (Buhler and Hetzer, 1927) in which we found that active babies showed curiosity and a certain courage in tackling new stimuli as well as aggressiveness in getting things, while babies who were afraid and withdrew from new stimuli showed a more passive behavior.

Can we then, on the basis of all these data conclude that the active, outgoing baby "anticipates" a "positive" reality, that is, one in which he can operate expansively, while the passive, more withdrawing infant "anticipates" a "negative" reality, that is, one which is frightening and potentially harmful? When we say that the infants seem to have these anticipatory attitudes from the "beginning," we mean the attitudes are "congenital," not necessarily innate, because much may happen in the gestatory period. These anticipatory attitudes may, of course, be changed by experience.

74

Primary aggressiveness or passivity, a high or low activity level may then predispose an individual to move into the world as a place in which to be *active* and to *expand* or else as a place in which to be on the *defensive* and to *limit* himself. In being active and expansive, an individual would be able to pursue the satisfaction of his needs and/or to become creative in his environment. In being more defensive and self-limiting, an individual would primarily hold up his internal order and/or try to fit himself adaptively into his environment.

These four tendencies were hypothesized as *basic tendencies* by the author in a theoretical discussion (1959) and in the introduction to this book (see p. 15). It was reasoned that every individual has to be at all times need-satisfying, creative, adaptive, and order upholding, but that different individuals predominantly tend in the one or the other of these directions.

While assumed to appear in a congenitally given pattern, of which the generally observed congenital activity and aggression levels give evidence, it is not postulated that the pattern is unchangeable. On the contrary, it is quite likely that experiences may enhance one or the other tendency throughout a person's lifetime, with the reservation, however, that the earlier experiences are the more decisive. As Eiduson, Eiduson, and Geller point out in summarizing the experimental work of many authors, "the evidence suggests that habits formed in early life are persistent in adult behavior, that later perceptual capacities seem to be structured by early experiences, and that there seem to be certain stages in ontogeny during which certain types of behavior normally are molded and shaped for life" (p. 11 f.).

This basic disposition pattern and the earliest experience would then make one individual more apt to be shaped by

75

the environment than another. The primarily need-satisfying, impulsive individual and the primarily creative person will pursue what they want to have and to do no matter where they are, unless they are completely overpowered and crushed. The primarily adaptive individual on the other hand will allow the environment to influence or to determine his direction.[3]

Our rapidly advanced civilization and century has provided us with sad examples of overpowering group impacts on individuals. We could see on the one hand the easily adaptable immigrants to foreign countries, individuals who let themselves be acculturated and absorbed by new cultural environments at age levels where usually one does not expect such flexibility. On the other hand, we have seen the wearing-down of creative persons' initiative if they were not adaptive enough to the conditions of their new cultural environment. The breaking of independent spirits has been cruelly demonstrated in concentration camps, where, on the other hand, some persons were able to find themselves and to preserve an absolutely astounding integrity. (See V. E. Frankl, 1959a.)

Individuals unable to keep up their internal order under the impact of an overpowering, uncongenial environment, are found to fall apart in schizoid distintegration or in with-

---

3. It is important to note that the four basic tendencies are not thought of as separate entities without dynamic interaction. It is evident that there is interaction, similar to dynamic processes in other areas. Cognitive and affective processes are for example two distinctly different approaches to reality, yet there are mutual influences between them. These influences vary from one individual to another and there is a varying predominance of the cognitive or the affective factor.

Exemplification of dynamic interaction between the basic tendencies would lead us off the present subject. But as a brief notation we may mention that the creative output of a person who lets himself be influenced by his environment will be quite different from that of a person who tries to keep himself free from such influence and so on. Examples will later contribute more concrete material to these considerations.

drawal attempts at self-protection. This last observation refers to case examples that will be discussed subsequently.

In short, the contention is that, depending on the pattern of an individual's basic tendencies and selectivity, his environment, in an individually varying manner, influences his development. While it is evident that the individual cannot help but utilize the available circumstances into which he is born, he can be selective within the given frame and may, if creative, impose his own stamp on his environment.

In concluding our survey, we might hypothesize that the multiple determinants of the self and of values would be found first in a genetic setup that becomes active in a given environment with selectivity due to individual differences of potentialities and sensitivity and of which we might think in terms of a "core" or "rudimentary self"; secondly, however, this gets instantly, that is, right from the start, changed through interaction with a given environment, which becomes immediately a codeterminant of the individual's development; thirdly, we find a congenital pattern of basic tendencies of which activity and sensitivity levels give evidence and that in turn have been established to offer a pretty reliable basis for the prediction of later patterns of psychological functioning.

3 The Self and Values in Human Development

1.
The Problem of the Self and Values in Human Development

It seems to me that in spite of many differences of opinion regarding the definition of the self, it is generally thought of as the representative of the "whole person." Whatever this whole person may be conceived of is not easy to say. But I believe most psychologists would agree that normally the whole person should participate in the process of human development and that something or other is wrong if parts of the person are left behind.

But how do we conceive of *human development?* Here we are in the greatest of dilemmas. The elaborate Freudian theory of development, which actually covers only the beginning of life, the schematic developmental framework of Sullivan, the information derived from his as well as all the other analytic groups' clinical evidence, the information derived from the tremendous material amassed over half a century by child psychologists and their theoretical outlines, the more recent collections of data assembled by social anthropologists that are nearly as tremendous—all stand as a massive body of evidence. On the other hand, the lack of developmental research by the self-realizationists whom one would consider most committed to the idea of demonstrating self-realization in its initial phases leaves us in a state of confusion. Where do we stand with all this disparate thinking and all this factual knowledge?

In the field of attempts at integration of theoretical thinking and material information, we find many psychologists at work who try to relate anthropological findings to child psychological material and we find many sociologists trying to test the Freudian and other theories in applying them to their data. No one as yet has seen all these things in relation to one another and probably no single person will be able to accomplish this vision in the near future.

Mussen and Conger (1956) have from the child psychologists' point of view, recently tried more comprehensively than others to integrate the diverse materials. The reasons why they do not help us here are that they do not enter into a discussion of value development, that their definition of the self is debatable, and that of course they do not handle the whole of human development. Mead and Wolfenstein's (1954) book *Childhood in Contemporary Cultures* emphasizes cultural more than the developmental aspect. The available books on human development do not as yet integrate dynamics with factual information.

Erikson's recent study, *Identity and the Life Cycle* (1959) is outstanding in many respects and represents a great step forward in the direction of an over-all integration of the numerous aspects involved. He does justice to dynamic, developmental, and cultural-anthropological data. Some of his concepts, like "self-sameness" and "trust," can no more be excluded from child psychology.

My main difficulty with Erikson's developmental scheme as outlined in his life cycle studies is that I do not see the nature of the eight categories whose development is hypothesized. Erikson says they are systematically related but he does not say, to my knowledge, what system they represent: functional, behavioral, attitudinal, or dynamic. If they are goals or some kind of tendencies, I do not see their common denominator.

I am also unclear about the connection between this concept of ego development and the rest of the Freudian system.

A final objection is that I do not believe that all progress in the psychosocial, or in any part of human development, is at all times due to crises, important as the aspect of crises may be. I do not think that there are always crises connected with progress like, for example the beginning of walking, talking, becoming a group member, entering formal education, getting a job for the first time, having sex relationships for the first time, and so on although in some individuals these advances are accomplished only after going through a crisis.

Erikson's attempt to outline a system of ego development was a response to requests from groups who were aware that for our orientation in education as well as in psychotherapy we are badly in need of such a frame of reference.

In view of this need, specifically when it comes to the

handling of value problems, I will briefly present a *developmental scheme* of my own, although I make no claim of its completeness or finality.

Before I do this, I will state however once more how I define values, self, and ego.

"Values" are *preferred goals*. The preference may be factual or normative, that is, it may derive from any level of our personality.

The "self" is the *core* of the whole person. I think of this core as a *system* as well as a *process*. The process I see much in the same way as Erikson so aptly describes it, a process having direction. The direction is toward fulfillment via integrated operation of the four basic tendencies of self. They represent the system. In their operation a selective organization of goals takes place in a hierarchical order. Examples of the integration of these four basic tendencies are cited later in the discussion of clinical material (see pp. 136 ff.).

The self can become conscious. In the sphere of consciousness, it is called the *phenomenal self*. The dynamic relationship between the core self and the phenomenal self is not as yet really known. The effect that our phenomenal self has on the outlook of our "real" self is seemingly often slanted, in consequence of conscious ideals regarding one's own personality. The description of this distortion was one of Karen Horney's eminent merits.

The phenomenal self is a creation of the *ego*, or better, it is a function of the ego. This subsystem of the whole personality whose modes of operation have not necessarily become clearer by means of the enormously increased literature about it, seems to set up goal preferences of its own. These values are the result of the ego's outlook on reality.

How the ego's value development and the underlying core-self's value development relate, materially and theoretically, seems to me still completely problematical. Karen Horney has shown certain aspects of these processes, but we do not yet have any developmental outline.[1]

2.
Developmental Origins of the Self

If we ask ourselves how the core-self originates and how the first values are established in the individual, we might go back to what was discussed in the previous section. We saw there that the genetic setup's initial interaction with the environment begins with its primary activity and selectivity. In the newborn infant we find from the start congenital activity degrees (Fries, 1937, 1953) and we find other signs of directivity and selective reactions. There are forerunners of *identification* in imitation, there are preferences, curiosity, and interests, as I have described in another place in more detail (1961).

The question is whether all these behaviors of the infant represent only scattered, internally unrelated responses with the only goal being to re-establish *homeostasis* as some writers assume. I personally do not believe that at any time of the human being's existence, except in pathological conditions, the re-establishing of homeostasis is ever a goal. As was discussed by this author (1959) and by many other recent writers, homeostasis is not a goal, but only a condition of functioning. The goal always lies in accomplishments beyond the here and now of homeostasis.

1. Inasmuch as self-realization is the goal of one of the basic tendencies I postulate, my outline of stages belongs in that frame.

If then we assume goal-setting tendencies toward certain accomplishments from the start, the question still remains as to when *one over-all directivity* is detectable in which the infant's self would seem unified and express itself.

Erik Erikson is of the opinion that at the beginning the infant's identity is established in his *trust*, which would be a carrier as it were of the individual's continuity and self-sameness. The child that is made to distrust, would have nothing to rely on and would be thrown hither and yon in his feelings.

This trust then would be an inner condition implying a receptiveness and a *looking forward* to good things to come, things that would enhance the baby's existence, would be upbuilding or what we defined in the foregoing chapter as "constructive."

This basic trust indeed represents the most basic "belief" with which the healthy baby moves forward into the world. This belief as it were, is his first identity, but it is one that includes an expectation. What is it that the baby expects? Or better, what expectation lies built-in in trust? Some people seem to find that the answer to that is simple; they feel trust asks for reassurance, and it is *love* and *care* that provide this. True, love and care are basic, so basic that as Bowlby (1952) and Spitz (1945) have shown in their comprehensive studies, their absence has disastrous effects.

But basic as they are, are love and care all the baby is looking forward to, or all the baby's self is directed toward? To me the baby's trust encompasses the whole of that world into which he finds himself born and into which he moves with the expectation as it were, not only to get love and care, but also—and I would say nearly as much so—of being active and *doing things*. B. Mittelmann (1954) establishes

83

the concept of a motor urge or drive that follows a developmental scheme.

Observations of infants who are tied for the whole first year to the cradle board, and who on top of that—as Lotte Danzinger and Liselotte Frankl (1943) found in the case of Albanian mountain tribes—are for six months kept most of the time in a dark corner of a mud hut show that none of the love and care these babies get can make up for their frustrated activity needs. These babies, who cannot move around, not even move their hands, who have nothing to look at, and only the mother's voice to listen to, get so frustrated that they cry all the time and only through the mother's continuous rocking of their cradle are put into a kind of daze and hypnotic sleep.

These children, when brought out of their confinement and offered age-adequate toys and other stimuli, were completely listless and as apathetic as Spitz's hospitalized infants. And yet these babies had love. But "love is not enough" as Bettelheim told us years ago. The confined baby wants the opportunity for a beginning of *self-realization in activities* and it is part of his trust that he will find this.

No self-expression emerges from these hostile or apathetic children who were traumatized by either lack of love or complete deprivation of self-actualizing opportunities. These children have lost an essential part of their selves, namely the potential for self-actualization or creative expansion. Either this potential was killed in the bud or else it could only be reawakened in long and deep psychotherapy. These hostile or apathetic children become the people who, once they become aware of their problem, will forever go around questioning what their real self is, who and what they really are, and what they really want. This is what we hear so often

84

in psychotherapy from people who to lesser degrees have also been traumatized in their initial self-development.

On the other hand, the receiving of love may be instrumental in encouraging the infant to move actively out into the world and use his freedom. This might be hypothesized, in view of Harlow's (1958, 1960) observations with monkey infants who were raised without mothers (or mother-substitutes to which they could cling) and did not manipulate nor explore the field.

Shall we then define the origin of the real self as that identity emerging out of an adequately rewarded trust, both insofar as the receiving of love and care as well as the beginning self-actualization opportunities are concerned?

With this definition we have the initial self established with its two first directions. The tendencies to need-satisfaction and to creative expansion seem to evolve right from the conception. But this description of initial directions appears not to be complete.

We found newborn infants equipped with the ability to respond to sensory stimuli and to manifest perceptual sensitivity of different degrees as well as to produce reactions of contagion and of imitative identification with people. This behavior gives evidence from the beginning of a *selective reactivity*, indicative of an individually structured learning process.

But there is more. Within days after birth, *coordinative and integrative activities* set in. As for example, Ripin and Hetzer (1930) have shown in their studies of newborn babies' responses in the feeding situation that elimination of disturbing movements already occurs from the second and third meal on and new helpful movements are produced after a few days.

In the early sound imitations of the four- to eight-weeks-old infant, one observes an intense struggle of tongue and mouth to produce the accurate sound.

What is the direction of these endeavors and these accomplishments that, if successful, always seem to result in facial or vocal expressions of satisfaction? It seems to me that here we observe from the start a *self-regulative adaptivity* at work.

Furthermore, it seems to me that we observe from a few days after birth on a satisfaction that is of a different kind than the satiation satisfaction or the satisfaction after creatively expansive play movements. The well-coordinated and integrated action of successful feeding or imitating is an *orderly* procedure resulting in *mastery*.

In descriptions of psychotic children's failure to accomplish these earliest coordinations and integrations, we get a good countercheck to the unification that the normal child achieves. Lauretta Bender (1952), for example, finds in many schizophrenic children's infancies a lack of coordination and complete unrelatedness. Annemarie Weil (1953, 1956) describes the lack of structure or focus, the diffuseness of reaction, the overload of anxieties in a number of cases in which she can trace its origin back to early infancy, to "the dawn of ego development."

Excessive anxiety is obviously the result of these failures at adaptation and at establishing an *inner order* of experiences. While prepared in preconscious dispositions, as for example in continuous hypersensitive reactions that keep the infant in continuous imbalance, the disorder becomes particularly evident on the ego level of development. This is the level on which coordinations and integrations are accomplished and the personality's relatedness, internally and to the outside world, is established in an adapted and orderly way.

Summarizing our observations up to this point, we can say that we found the healthy infant directively active from the start. With a fundamental belief, beginning with trust, this infant moves into the world, displaying a few days after his birth distinct signs of orientation in the direction of need satisfaction, creative expansion, self-limiting adaptation, and order upholding tendencies.

Our theoretical assumption was that there is an over-all end-goal of *fulfillment* toward which the individual strives in a united, but individually patterned directivity of these tendencies. The individual patterning results from pre-dominances of one or the other tendency. The goal as we find it in the adult may be envisaged more in terms of "happiness," or lasting accomplishments, or self-integration into the order of things, or inner harmony and peace.

The goal-value orientation of the first ten months I consider essentially preconscious. I believe that at about eight to ten months of age self-awareness sets in, and with this, the phenomenal self comes into action. We enter the phase of consciousness of values and of the beginning of self-evaluation.

3.

Beginnings of the Phenomenal Self

"Consciousness is," as Piaget (1954) has said, "essentially a system of meanings that may be *cognitive* (perceptual, conceptual, etc.) or *affective* (values with a conative factor being implied here). These two, cognitive and affective

87

aspects of meaning always go together; none is present without the other, although they may be examined separately" (p. 145).

Applied to the self, Piaget's observation might call our attention to the fact that various phases of self-awareness are probably accompanied by corresponding affective and conative aspects of self-development. Most research, of which Ruth Wylie (1961) gives a comprehensive critical survey, seems to focus exclusively on either the perceptual and conceptual side or else on the motivational side of self-experience, as evidenced in problems of self-acceptance, self-regard, self-esteem, self-adequacy, and the like.

None of the available studies seems to investigate the relationship between the cognitive and the affective aspects of the self, especially not their origins in the child.

It seems to me from tentative observations that perceptual and affective experiences precede the beginnings of conceptual and conative experiences of the self.

I see the rudimentary beginnings or antecedents of self-awareness at the age of about eight to ten months, possibly even earlier. Quite striking to the observer is the moment, when a nine- to ten-month-old baby discovers his face in the mirror and begins to investigate the image he beholds with astonishment. I also find an inkling of self-awareness in the eight-month-old-baby's reactions during the peek-a-boo play situation, when at his reappearance from under the cloth the mother exclaims: "Ah, there is my baby."

The impression is normally that of a happy surprise. I noticed a similar look in the eyes of five-month-old-babies when they suddenly by accident, meet the look of another baby that sits near them, but that up to now seemed some undefined meaningless object.

This first dawning of one's own and somebody's else's *identity* seems to be experienced as a kind of "aha!" as Karl Buhler has called these experiences and described in the discovery of object-relationships. Phenomenal identity would seem then in the beginning to occur as a self-perception simultaneous with the perception of the other person as person.

The assumption that the first relationship of oneself to oneself is perceptual, accompanied by an affect, would fit well with the established fact that the first relationships among objects as discovered around this same age are also perceptual. This has been shown in many experiments.

The *affect* in this discovering of the self would be, I suppose, just as good or as bad as the feeling about one's functioning and/or the relationships with people, are at the time. I noticed that some five- to six-month-old babies would cry when they became aware of another baby near them. In most cases, however, I noticed smiling.

The distinction of the strange face as such takes place at around eight months and often causes what Spitz has called the eight-months' anxiety. This anxiety seems to me to have to do with the same dawning awareness of different identities. I do not find it equally strongly developed in all babies. The effect seems to be here estrangement.

I am not able to see that the child's awareness of himself originates, as some psychologists believe, necessarily in *experiences of disapproval*. It was Sullivan who saw the basis of anxiety in this experience. Among the child psychologists Mussen and Conger (1956) seem of this opinion.

It is usually assumed that during toilet training the child first becomes aware of approval and disapproval. While some mothers begin with toilet training extremely early, it does not generally occur before eight to ten months of age at the earliest. Mussen and Conger, who compared data on this, found that the earliest age at which toilet training is started is with the Tanalas of Madagascar, who begin anal training at two to three months and punish an infant for accidents after it is six months old. Mussen and Conger do not give average ages for these practices in our culture, but recommend eighteen months as the age when the child would be "ready" for it.

It seems to me that any habit formation taught during the first six to eight months of life must take place as a conditioned-reflex type of training without any self-awareness coming into the picture. The earliest self-awareness seems to me possible only at the aforementioned age of eight to ten months, during which the first object relationships are recognized and during which the first learning with "insight" into object relationships takes place. The occasion *can* then be, but need not be a situation of approval and disapproval as becomes evident from the examples I have given.

To these examples can be added another early source of identity experiences, that is the early *role play*. The earliest role play was observed by me at eleven months, again within the same period.

A little boy, for example, dusts a chair with a piece of paper, copying his mother; a little girl throws herself on her bed, closes her eyes and says "baba" which means, "I play now sleeping."

Two months later, both these children play at "smoking" by walking up and down while holding little sticks in their mouths and puffing "smoke" from time to time.

In these early *identifications* of which we find forerunners in imitation of sounds and movements from two months on,

90

there seems to be normally neither conflict nor trauma nor reaction to disapproval, but an expansive self-development.

One might already speak here of precursory stages to operations of modeling in the sense in which Bronfenbrenner (1958) defines it as in evidence if there is "some indication of striving on the part of one person to resemble another" (p. 128). The other is at this stage not as yet necessarily being experienced as an ideal. The child models himself after the grown-ups because it wants to be able to do what they do.

While these may be called *introjections* in the psychoanalytic sense, they seem not to be as yet introjections in replacement of Oedipal wishes. About the origins of the *self-picture* which arises out of a complex matrix of processes we can only make conjectures. The self-picture is partially determined by the experience of that "emotional climate" between mother and child that Spitz (1957) described in so masterly a way. In this emotional climate the newborn child feels himself beheld as beloved and precious or else perhaps as worthless and a burden, and so on. In mutual responses to tenseness and ease, roughness and gentleness of handling as described by Escalona (1949) and by Brody (1956), in the exchange of smiles and sounds first *interaction* gives a more substantial structure to the first *relationships* as well as to the *self-feeling* (C. Buhler [in press]).

Into this then is woven gradually that "egocentric participation" that Piaget (1951) describes and that makes the child perceive all events as due to willful actions into which he feels drawn as a participant and perhaps as the center.

And out of all this emerges with increasing impact that *introjection* and *projection*, which dynamic psychology has demonstrated appear in healthy as well as pathological manifestations.

A very sensitive description of how the earliest *introjection* and simultaneous *projection* take place and lead to an "expansion of the self" (James) while it is still in the process of being set up, is given by Murphy (1947). Murphy raises the question of whether the small child has a "working conception of the whole self before he begins to assimilate this self-picture to the picture of other persons" or whether he makes "affectively charged responses" jointly to parts of himself and to parts of another person, while "a partial assimilation of the self to others is under way" (p. 491). I would suppose, like Murphy, that the latter is true and that therefore from its start, "selfhood is interwoven with experiencing other individuals." His mother, father, brother, and sister become partly himself and he becomes partly them.

Into this first self-image becomes ingrained, so it seems from all evidence a perception of oneself as "beloved," "good," "clever," or else as the "not wanted," "disapproved," "stupid" person. An image of which the lucky and the unlucky ones see themselves often forever after.

Thus Linda, whom we will later introduce as one of those rare individuals whose childhood and further development were essentially happy and healthy, remembers from earliest days this glad feeling of being "beloved," "worthwhile," "approved of," that her mother gave to all her children.

Sally, on the other hand, one of my most unfortunate patients, who was raised in a slum in an atmosphere of hate and depravity, remembers that she never knew anything else about herself than the most negative attributes. She was always called "a bad child" and became convinced that she was. Her mother also made no secret out of the fact that she had not wanted her at all, because there were already too many mouths to feed in this house. She was called "stupid" whenever she made a mistake or got in her mother's way. Actually Sally was a highly intelligent girl as became evident in her later career. But she could not believe it for a long time, nor could she think of herself as anything but basically a "low" type of person, regardless of the unfathomable degree of integrity and honesty that she developed in opposition to *her background*.

But we are getting ahead of ourselves, since we should discuss this development in its different stages from its beginnings.

Clearly, *conscious self-awareness* as well as the setting up of ideals, both in terms of the *superego* as well as *ego ideals*, takes place at around two years of age or a little before. This is the stage in which the word and concept of "I" are acquired and in which begins, what Erikson so aptly calls, *"the battle for autonomy."*

4.

Stages of Self and Value Development in Childhood and Adolescence

Anybody who speaks of stages or phases must first protect himself against the reproach that he thinks in terms of discontinuous steps, when development is a continuous process. Naturally it is continuous. But in spite of all the gradualness with which changes take place, there comes a moment where a new ability or disability not only manifests itself, but changes the whole pattern of operations, often drastically. Such drastic changes take place when the child begins to walk and discovers a whole new world in walking around. Such changes take place when the child begins to talk, and they certainly also take place when the child discovers himself as a person and the good and bad that is being ascribed to persons, in fact with which they are being identified.

"Is he good boy, is he bad boy?" reflects Tobie at two. "No, he is bad boy," he decides with great satisfaction over his declaration. Temporarily at least, he chooses the identity and the values of the bad boy. This happens during the crisis period between one and a half and four, which Erikson aptly calls, "the battle for autonomy." In this period the child lives through those conflicts between obedience and willfulness, those first realizations that things are expected of him, those first pangs of conscience and guilt, and the anxiety that he may lose the love of the ones he needs the most if he does not identify with their demands—in short, all those complex and essentially unhappy experiences normally resulting in two things: one, the child identifies more or less willingly with his parents' ideas of right or wrong and of how he *ought* to behave; two, the child has discovered also that there are certain things that he is free to do on his own and that there are *choices* for him to make.

In identifying with his parents, the child incorporates their ideals, and thus the *superego* is born, which as Mussen and Conger (1956) reflect is to be considered the major product of identification, even if the Oedipus complex is not accepted as universal. They define identification as "a learned drive to imitate or to be like another individual (or individuals) to whom one is *emotionally attached*"[2] (p. 240).

But identification is so much more than this. As we have shown in the previous section, there are imitations of other persons, long before identification on the basis of an emotional attachment develops. In fact, a few weeks after the

2. Italics the author's.

94

infant is born, it begins to imitate sounds and movements with all signs of a real struggle for the right coordinations.

It seems to me that in these imitations, this "modeling," as Bronfenbrenner defines it, we have from almost the beginning of life first an inculcation of movements and behavioral habits, and later ideas and principles, by means of which *cultural identification* takes place. This is the acquisition of those basic orientations provided by culture that A. I. Hallowell (1954) listed as self and object orientation, spatiotemporal orientation, motivational orientation, and a sense of normative standards and values.

In this area of modeling, where culturally identifying habits, customs, and ideas are acquired, we may often observe play and learning processes based on adaptive tendencies or on interest, rather than always on emotional attachment or on admiration of an ideal.

If the Balinese baby, for example, as Margaret Mead (1955) describes it, learns movements more "from the feel of other people's bodies and from watching" than through verbal directions, which are rare, this cultural identification has nothing to do with emotions or ideals. It is in Mead's words, "a plastic adaptation."

But if, on the other hand, the bracelet-waving baby happens to hurt someone with his banging movement, and if then he is told "Isama is harsh," the baby is expected to gather gradually that its action is being judged. Thus, here we have a superego ideal come into the picture.

But there is a third element—identification by *choice*. Choice to me is the basis of the *ego-ideal*. This is an identification on neither the basis of an *emotional attachment* nor of *imitative responsiveness* to what the grown-ups or any others do, but on the basis of one's *own preferences*.

The question arises as to what exactly this identification

means and implies. To define it, we must once more go back to the fact of *selectivity*, which we introduced in the last chapter. Selectivity, as we saw it, would from the start have a more complex orientation than the pursuit of "innate preferences" in Hilgard's (1951) sense or in Tinbergen's (1948) sense of "innate perceptual patterns." It would from the start be regulated by the primary *motivational tendencies* that we discussed.

But how exactly do these operate in selective responses and in choices?

Speaking developmentally, *selective responsiveness* is in operation from the beginning, while *choice* is a much later behavior. If in a selective response to certain foods or sounds or other stimuli, the newborn infant is either receptive or rejective, he is so depending on how his organism is geared to these stimuli, on how satisfying they are, or how he can or cannot adapt to them.

If in response to two toys offered to him, the eight-month-old baby, for the first time in his life, makes a choice in showing a consistent preference for one of them, he does this on the basis of *comparison*. This becomes noticeable, in that his glance may go back and forth from one to the other before he grasps.

In this preference, a new determining factor seems to become manifest. This eight-month-old baby seems often to choose that toy with which he can do the most, that rattle he can swing better, that ball he can squeeze best, that animal he likes to hug.

The tendencies to creative expansion and in the direction of self-actualization begin to prevail here. Of course, other motives, like enjoyment of a pretty color or fear of too loud a rattle, may also come into play. But the *realiza-*

tion of one's own potentialities already becomes the manifest major concern of the child who would be, even at this early age, a "good chooser" in Maslow's terms.

The question is, of course, to what degree environmental influences permit or enhance this development. How freely can the individual's choices develop? This probably varies a great deal with different cultural traditions.

Interesting examples for this are given in Mead and Wolfenstein's (1955) book. As highly typical, we may note Martha Wolfenstein's observation of French children in a park.

She describes these playing children with their mothers and governesses. .The over-all picture is that they are constantly and consistently restrained in all their movements and activities. How do these children ever practice freedom? She describes them, squatting at their mothers' feet, never touching the ground, playing with sand, but never dirtying anything except their fingers, often dressed in elegant, unwashable clothes, never allowed to exchange or share toys with another child, never permitted to run around wildly, to shout, or to express themselves in any which way.

The same repressive training goes on at home and at school, the basic idea being that "childhood is not for fun," but for education.

This seems a cultural pattern in which all freedom of self-expression is condemned, and one would expect it to become forever repressed. Yet the adult French seem to enjoy life more than many other national groups and their creative self-expression in art has always been of the freest. How can we understand this?

Perhaps a partial explanation is that not all preparation for self-realization and setting up of ego-ideals must necessarily find immediate expression in actions. I have been able in some of my clinical cases, to trace the unexpressed beginning of later very effective ideals back to the fourth year of life.

From their reports, there is no doubt, that here are identifications and self-determination in the direction of realization of potentialities, and not identifications based on emotional attachments or merely imitative responses.

Myrna, now a forty-year-old woman, remembers in psychotherapy, that when she was four, she had found her ideal. It was a neighbor lady whom she had come to admire greatly in the course of a friendly relationship that developed between them. The occasion was the birthday of Myrna's mother. Myrna wanted to give her mother a present that she had made herself. The neighbor to whom she happened to tell this, suggested that she would show the little girl how to embroider a doily for her mother. This she did, and for a few weeks, Myrna found herself sitting in her neighbor's handsome living room, where she was entertained with cookies and fruit juice while embroidering her doily.

From then on, Myrna kept the ideal that she would become the same type of "nice lady" as the neighbor was. Simultaneously with her admiration for this lady, Myrna loved both her parents. In fact, she was quite close to her gentle and kind father. For her mother, who, compared with Myrna, was a rather passive and colorless person, the little girl harbored a kind of protective affection.

The image of the neighbor on the other hand was kept alive by Myrna, who later became a well-known dress designer.

Another example is the case of Celia, who at fifty-two remembered in psychotherapy how one day at four it became clear to her that she wanted to be like her aunt Elinore, who was "gay and pretty" and not like her mother who was always "sad and serious." This child was also emotionally

98

attached to her mother, but she did not identify with her. And again, this early self-determination survived many later temporary ideals. Celia discovered early that the "gay and pretty" aunt was rich and had married a man who adored her, while her mother who was "sad and serious" was not adored by Celia's father and did not have much money. Celia decided, to follow her aunt's footsteps, which she did, with a belated awakening to the fact, that she was although "gay" and "rich," not at all "happy."

Of course, somebody might now say that perhaps these two were neurotics, and therefore they developed a split between love and identification. This objection is, however, not valid.

While Myrna was an insecure and Celia a selfish child, their freedom of choice was at that point not yet impaired, as it became years later. Children who at this stage show definite neurotic trends, make choices that are not based on their potentials, but on other factors.

Roger, for example, at four years of age makes the decision "never to make a mistake again." This happened when his mother once again sent him from the table to wash his hands for dinner. Roger, who from his early years was as sensitive to criticism as he remained all through his life, became from the moment of his decision a compulsive perfectionist.

Of particular interest here is the example of a well-adjusted person; one of those who is usually less available for our studies because they do not often avail themselves of the longer analytic procedures, which seem to be the only technique deep enough to penetrate to these long-forgotten, early experiences. Neither questionnaire studies nor longer-term interview studies yield, in my experience, the same results. By "analytic" I mean incidentally not necessarily "psychoanalytic" in the strict sense, but any of those long-term explorative procedures that various psychotherapy schools have developed.

The normal case I wish to discuss is that of a social worker who in conjunction with her professional training underwent a long-term analytic procedure.

Linda, as we will call her, will be discussed at some length in this and the following chapters. Her history is given in part at the end of this chapter and in Chapter 4. At this point, we are interested in some of her feelings at the age of four regarding certain "ideals" she began, one might say, to be set on. They distinctly formed two groups. One group were those things her very beloved mother liked her to do. They were the wish to be clean, she disliked being dirty; the wish to please and to help her mother, and to do things just right. All these might be called superego ideals.

But then she had certain ideals of her own. In this family of a ranch manager, in which intellectual interests were not particularly enhanced, Linda's curiosity and inquisitiveness made her want *to know and to learn* whatever she got a hold of. She had her two-year-older brother teach her what he learned in school and she tried to teach her two-year-younger brother, because she thought these things were so interesting.

Linda even as a baby had been curious and alert, says her mother. Thus, her intense interest in learning, which continuously represented Linda's ideal, was probably more her own than developed through identification, although her older schoolgoing brother might have functioned as a model for her. He might anyway have enhanced her own interests. She says she was always proud of him, and they always got along beautifully.

One other ideal of Linda's at this age seems particularly interesting to me, in view of most children's suffering during the "autonomy battle." Linda, it seems, was given quite early by her understanding mother the awareness of her "rights as a person." It seems the mother defined very successfully for the little girl when she was about three to four years old the idea that everybody has certain rights and certain duties. Linda thought a lot about having rights. She distinctly remembers making one of the applications of this idea at four years of age when she overheard her mother saying to her brother in the next room that if a lady came into the room he was to get up and offer her his chair. Promptly, she marched into the room and insisted he offer her his chair, since she was a lady.

This ideal of every person's rights stayed consistently with Linda and became one of her strongest motivations in later political work. It is an idea in which she obviously identified with her mother's thinking, but not on a superego, but on an ego-ideal level.

The example of Linda shows how complex the motivational pattern regarding ideals seems to be already at four years of age; ideals that incidentally, while ordinarily they sink into oblivion as far as conscious memory is concerned, are much more persistent than many later conceived goals.

The scanty research material and the techniques used until now with respect to this whole problem of motivation are not as yet geared to its complexity. Ruth Wylie in her comprehensive literary survey actually quotes only one study that concerns itself with the question of the child's ideals regarding himself.

Havighurst, Robinson, and Dorr (1946) compare compositions written by children of six to eight and of eight to sixteen years written about "The person I would like to be like." They found that while from six to eight the parents or some family member was the typical choice, there is after eight a trend away from the family. From eight to sixteen there was a trend toward choosing a glamorous person, then a visible adult, and finally a composite, imaginary person.

A study of J. B. Winker (1949) by means of interview questions had similar results.

In experimenting with a questionnaire approach myself, I came to the conclusion that in direct questioning one does not get at what children really feel. Partly, they don't dare to say it, partly, they don't know themselves. These things become clear often only in longer psychotherapy or interview procedures.

Incidentally, if for Havighurst, Robinson, and Dorr "parents and other family members" comprise one category, they do not seem to consider the possibility that a preference of "other family members" implies more often than not a rejection of the child's own parents as ideal. Celia's case was an example of this.

Ruth Munroe (1955) in discussing the problem of identification, makes very realistic observations in her criticism of the cliché of parents as ideals, which in her opinion does not apply in America because here the younger generation lives almost typically a strikingly different life from the pattern set by the parents. She thinks that perhaps in Freud's Vienna this was different. Perhaps it was. But I can assure her that the Europeans of this century have become by and large just as critical of their parents' shortcomings as Americans. The difference is not one between two Western subcultures, but between generations. This I have shown in *Three Generations in Adolescent Diaries* (1934). I showed in a survey of sixty-one girls' and forty-two boys' diaries written by adolescents born in the years between 1830 and 1915, including five diaries from the United States, the enormous differences of three generations' attitudes to various factors of life. The observations, which were carried out in detail in four extensively quoted sample diaries, led to the conclusion that in that total period of seventy-five years with undoubtedly gradual changes, rather pronounced transformations can be found twice; first in diaries of adolescents born between 1880 and 1890 as against the generation before; a second time in those born between 1906 and 1916.

One of the main areas of change is in the attitude to the family. The representative of the first of these three generations belongs without any doubt as an integral member of his family. Parents are central figures in these adolescents' lives, they are called "beloved," are constantly considered, admired, and quoted as authorities and as examples.

In the second of the three generations, the family's authority is still valid, but a new striving for independence and ideals that are greatly at variance with those of the parents results in serious clashes.

In the third of these generations, parents are discussed in a matter-of-fact way, with a nonpassionate independence, even when they are admired and praised.

Even more than those born around World War I, I find our present adolescents and young adults groping for their own identity, frequently without having even considered looking for anybody as model. The parents are often the furthest from their minds, when it comes to looking for models.

According to Sopchak (1952) and several other studies of *identification with parents*, low identification scores are associated with a tendency toward abnormality. If this were really a valid finding, a great many of our present-day young people would have to be abnormal. Bronfenbrenner (1958), who discusses these findings, doubts their validity. To me it seems that things are more complicated than they appear from these Q-studies.

While the superego-ideal is the result of an *adaptive* behavior, the ego ideal is a *creative and expansive* expression of the mental growth process, which generates a further new attitude. I have called this the discovery of the *task aspect*.

The concept of task was originally introduced into psychology by Ach (1905) and later modified by Lewin (1926). Ach speaks of it as a goal-presentation or *intention*, which is the source of a determining tendency toward the accomplishment of a certain goal. Lewin thinks of this as a "quasi-need-tension system." As Rapaport (1951) points out in referring to Gibson's (1941) discussions of the "set-concept," the motivation-effecting mechanisms of sets are still problematic, but probably should be thought of as interests, attitudes, or values.

Children are taught the attitude and value of certain accomplishments like cleanliness or orderliness in their early years. Since Freud, the effectiveness of these concepts is attributed to superego functions.

In our child psychological studies, we were always struck by the observation that at a certain point around five years of age well-developing children seem to produce a task concept of their own. They assign themselves tasks in their play —"This is hard work," says the five-year-old Bubi Scupin while building a bridge. Or, "Let me finish my work first," when he is called from play to wash hands for dinner.

This might of course simply be interpreted as a transferral of the superego task attitude to a play situation and the usage of the word "work" may here simply occur in the sense of role playing.

But the fact is that this attitudinal and thought pattern is not found before five years, and it always makes the impression on the observer of some genuine, new type of motivation. In tying it up with my previously mentioned data about autonomous ego-ideals, I would hypothesize that this task aspect develops in the wake of the child's first genuine value and goal setting at four.

In some children this *freeing of the task aspect* does not seem to take place. In some of my neurotic cases all tasks seem to remain forever superego-bound. I would therefore be ready to assume that the originating of a new task aspect on the ego-level of self-determination distinguishes the healthy from the neurotic development at this stage.

The autonomous value system of the self as it appears here freed on the ego-level, shows a further progress in the development of first attempts at *objective self-evaluation*.

Also, self-evaluations are early taught to the child. "Is he a bad boy or a good boy?" asks Tobie in talking loudly to himself. "No, he is a *bad* boy," he concludes his monologue with great satisfaction. This was when he was two. The child thinks here again entirely in terms of superego values. Tobie is just at a moment where he enjoys his rebellion.

This type of self-evaluation is highly emotional and completely defensive. "The teacher gave me a 'D,' because she does not like me," is a typical report of the beginner in school.

Personally, I did not expect nor find in my earlier studies the ability of objective self-evaluation before about eight years. But if Pauline Sears (1960), for example, already finds in the age group of six or seven self-appraisal that correlates with teachers' and test ratings, perhaps in this direction also today's children mature earlier.

While the progress of self development between about four and about eleven or twelve seems to me to be essentially a matter of mental growth, the adolescent period brings, as generally recognized, a severe crisis. The reason lies in the complexity of this period's "tasks of life," to use Havighurst's expression. The detachment from the family, the preparation of a role in society are required at a time when new needs rush in and when the individual feels himself faced with the problem of finding his way to a sex partner and to his sexual identity.

The realization of the break between the childhood life at home and the grown-up life that awaits him in the world makes every somewhat normal youngster rather thoughtful, unless an environment determined to prevent so much introversion keeps him from ever thinking about anything. To me, it seems the normal impulse of youth to *review* one's past and *preview* one's future, and to see oneself for the first time in a historical light, so much so that the youths would write an autobiography if ever they had time any more.

Rare is the youth who begins to successfully find himself in this period, so much the more as the older generation does practically nothing to help. It was interesting to me to read this sentence in P. Symonds' (1961) book:

> The general impression gained from reviewing the experiences of these twenty-eight individuals as they progressed from adolescence to young adulthood is that their maturing was on the whole a blind, trial-and-error process. Little or nothing has been done to help them to anticipate and plan the next steps. Every problem had to be met and dealt with whatever resources the individual had available when he came face-to-face with it. Formal education gave almost no help in preparing a person to meet the problems of education, vocation, and marriage that he must inevitably face (p. 206).

This is sad news in our so-enlightened time, when we consider ourselves to be so progressive.

With adolescence a *first life cycle* is closed and a *new life cycle* is started. The individual must now start out into life on his own and so must his self. As the love relationship between him and his parents laid the foundation for the infant's self-development, a new love relationship with a sex partner will lay a new foundation for the adolescent's self-development when he grows into adulthood. Thus, his detachment from childhood is simultaneous with his laying new foundations for his adult life.

At this point, the reader may like to turn to Tables 2 and 3, on which self-development appears tentatively and schematically related to ages as well as to the basic tendencies, depending on which is predominant in each phase. The various age levels are listed in the left-hand vertical column, and the basic tendencies and fulfillments may be read across the table. Twice the individual goes through the cycle from need-satisfaction to fulfillment of self. In the seventies, eighties, or nineties, as the case may be, another detachment takes place, the detachment from life itself, with a regression to attendance to needs till the end.

On Table 3, behavioral trends of the different periods are indicated tentatively. The different stages of fulfillment are interrupted by periods of disturbance in which usually no fulfillment is reached.

5.

Self-Development in Adulthood
and the End of Life-Fulfillment

Bugental (1960) finds that in referring to themselves, people mention their *name* as the most important first iden-

Table 2—Basic Tendencies and Development of Self

Ages	Need-satisfaction	Self-limiting adaptation	Creative expansion	Establishing of inner order	Fulfillment
Birth to 1½	Trust and love, evolvement and discovery of self-sameness				
1½ to 4		Learning of styles of life. Obedience and superego-ideal vs. independence, first absorption of culturally determined ideas			
4 to 8			Autonomous ego-ideals value setting, aspect of task		
8 to 12				Attempts at objective self-evaluation in social roles	
12 to 18	Sex needs and problem of sexual identity			Review and preview of self-development (Autobiography)	Fulfillment of and detachment from childhood
18 to 25 (30)		Tentative self-determination of role in society			
25 (30) to 45 (50)			Self-realization in occupation, marriage, and own family		
45 (50) to 65 (70)				Critical self-assessment	
65 (70) to 80 (85)					Self-fulfillment
80 (85) to death	Regression to predominant need-satisfaction				

Table 3—Basic Tendencies and Development of Self, Including Behavioral Trends

Ages	Need-satisfaction	Self-limiting adaptation	Creative expansion	Establishing of inner order	Fulfillment
Birth to 1½	Trust and love, evolvement and discovery of self-sameness	Coordination and adaptation of movements	Spontaneous activities	Beginning of integration of movements	Well-being
1½ to 4	Pregenital sex, attachment to parents	Learning of styles of life. Obedience and superego-ideal vs. independence, first absorption of culturally determined ideas	Role play and artistic creativity	Superego conscience and first patterning of ideas	
4 to 8	Latency period	Acceptance of membership role in family, learning of culturally determined ideas	Autonomous value setting, ego-ideals aspect of task	Self-appraisal regarding ego ideals and of culturally determined ideas	Accomplishment
8 to 12	Latency period	Acceptance of role and assignment in school and culturally determined education	Games, sport, group mentally explorative activities	Attempts at objective self-evaluation in social roles	
12 to 18	Sex needs and problem of sexual identity	Independence vs. family domination	Personality development, love, intellectual spurt	Review and preview of self-development (Autobiography)	Fulfillment of and detachment from childhood
18 to 25 (30)	Sex needs and problem of sexual identity	Tentative self-determination of role in society	Occupational and love experiments	Search for self	
25 (30) to 45 (50)	Culmination of sex-love union	Acceptance of family and occupational role	Self-realization in occupation, marriage, and own family	Finding own self	Self-realization
45 (50) to 65 (70)	Climacteric and health problems	Self-denial for family; community, welfare obligations	Building up of estates and positions	Critical self-assessment	
65 (70) to 80 (85)	Concern with health	acceptance of limitations	Finishing off life work	Autobiographical retrospect	Self-fulfillment
80 (85) to death	Regression to predominant need-satisfaction	Acceptance of end of life approaching			

tifying characteristic. Incidentally, in child psychology we have always considered the step to identification by name as one of the most important in mental development. As Karl Buhler (1934) shows in his *Theory of Language*, the referral by name objectively establishes an object. The name is therefore the first attribute by which we are established. Bugental finds furthermore, that *sex* is an important attribute to youth, *age* seems to become more important at the peak of life and *occupation* as well as *family status* in more mature years.

If these findings were proved valid, they would show quite interestingly that the young person is first concerned with the establishment of his sexual identity. At the peak of life, we become age conscious, because we begin only then to realize the reality that soon we will be aging and then we will be gone. In the more mature years, our objective roles in family and community gain in importance. We identify more with our obligation, and as Frenkel and Weisskopf (1937) established, our duties take to a great extent the place of our wishes, or both can hardly be separated.

Fulfillment then seems to be aspired toward in terms of fulfillment of wishes and desires, as well as of obligations and accomplishments. The emphasis is first on the aspect of *desires*, later on the aspect of *accomplishments*.

This is the model of the healthy and successful development. If a person remains unsuccessful in the fulfillment of some basic wishes, he may not be able to progress to an adequate identification with the accomplishment aspect of life. Symonds (1961), for example, finds in his follow-up study of adolescents whom he saw again as young adults that unrealistic, wishful thinking increased in those who had had disappointments in life. In certain neurotic develop-

110

ments, Frenkel and Weisskopf found the reverse sequence of excessive concern with obligations in youth and belated preoccupation with unfulfilled desires in the climacteric years.

The *self-determination* of these goals I have described (1960) as a *tentative and experimental* one in the earlier adult years (eighteen to twenty-five or thirty) with a more *definite and specified* self-determination following on the peak of adulthood (thirty or thirty-five to forty-five or fifty). In this period, self-realization should begin to be experienced. In the climacteric phase (forty-five or fifty to sixty or sixty-five) *critical self-assessment* normally culminates. Even heretofore not very thoughtful persons may unexpectedly be overcome with feelings of guilt regarding the time they wasted or did not use in the most profitable way to obtain what they could have out of life, to accomplish what they should have, to provide security for their old age and a sense of fulfillment for their life as a whole.

One biography must suffice here in place of the many with which I have tried in two previous publications (1960, 1961) to illustrate the various phases of this self-development.

For a brief illustration of the sequence of these phases in an essentially healthy development, I am using the story of *Linda*, a woman now fifty-five, social worker, married, and who has one adolescent daughter. We mentioned her briefly in a previous section of this chapter.

Linda grew up on several California ranches that her father managed. The family being unable to give her the college education she was very interested in, she had to bide her time, till at nineteen an uncle offered her a job in his business in Hawaii.

In the next three years, Linda did a number of things, which we put under the heading of *experimental and tentative self-determination*. While staying at her relatives' home and making enough of a living at her clerical job to keep herself going, she started studying at the university, socialized, and dated and had her first sexual experience with a student she was very fond of. She thought of her future as one in which professional work and marriage should be combined. She also wanted a family. During this period she met a young man, who, a few years older than she, was on a magazine as writer and editor, and who asked her to marry him.

When at twenty-three Linda married Hal, she was willing to defer her further education and to devote herself to home-making and building a family. That is to say, she gave herself a *definite self-determination* and felt her *self-realization* would begin as a wife, mother, and homemaker.

It appeared then that Hal was not as yet ready for this same goal. She recognized only then that he was a rather insecure and socially maladjusted person. For several years, he denied her the child she wanted so much, and which he had promised her. He showed himself quite dependent on her help for his career and wanted her to finish her studies and help with the family income for a while, till he felt secure enough to found a family of his own.

Linda adjusted to this new program. She finished her undergraduate studies and got herself a job.

When at the end of her twenties, Hal still did not want children, and in other ways made life difficult for his wife, Linda considered divorce. At this time she met another man who appealed to her greatly. They considered marriage and had a short affair. In working things through for herself, Linda decided against divorce and this second marriage, because she felt her husband needed her more, their sexual and personal relationships were fulfilling in spite of his personality difficulties, and Jack, while attractive, did not share her many intellectual and cultural interests as her husband did.

Instead of divorcing Hal, she worked with concerted effort on his problems and their marriage and on the planning of a child, which she had at thirty-one.

This must be called actually a first kind of *self-assessment*, at least as far as the marriage was concerned.

Linda's next years were filled with raising her child, who had a number of serious illnesses, moving back to the United States, helping her husband with the problems of his new position and making new friends in a new environment. There was also a second pregnancy ending in an abortion.

The difficulties she had to overcome in these years brought Linda near a breakdown at around forty-four. The reasons were partly the continual harrassments by illnesses and Hal's personality difficulties, which threatened often to overcome even her optimistic and basically happy disposition, but she felt there was a further lack of fulfillment. In trying to analyze this for herself, she came to the conclusion that as a person she had not realized her full potential in breaking up not only her education and her career, but also in not having contributed her share to the solution of our time's social and cultural problems.

She decided to clarify her thinking further with the help of a psychotherapist with whom she had made friends, and after an *all-round self-assessment*, she went back to school, finished her education to the point of obtaining a higher degree, and got herself a position as a social worker in an agency in which she could contribute the kind of work that she believed in.

At this point then, the self-assessment of her forties resulted for this rare and courageous person in a retrieving for herself of the implements for the completion of her self-realization. Since at this point husband, child, and home were in good enough balance to allow for her absence and absorption in an occupation, she felt that she had now the rare opportunity to bring her life to a true fulfillment.

Climacteric problems, as is well known, often have more to do with the guilt feelings and regrets experienced in unfavorable self-assessments than with the biological problems of this phase.

The case of Ben, which is discussed in Chapter 5 under the aspect of a limited value potential, is an example of a defeat during the climacteric self-assessment. Ben felt he had wasted his life in a neurotic fight against his father. Instead of ever finding himself and pursuing his own goals, all he had done was to spite his father.

When now belatedly he tried to develop a talent as a writer that he had shown at certain occasions in previous years, he was no longer able to concentrate and to go to the effort that this type of mental work required.

The only value he could still bring to materialization was to love truly and for the first time in his life.

But in his belated struggle for creative self-realization he felt a failure and it was probably not quite accidental when he was run over by a car and died in this accident in his fifties.

Few people seem lucky enough to strike a positive balance when they assess themselves in their climacteric years. Some find it easier than others to resign themselves to their limited accomplishments. Some take up a redoubled struggle to complete what they feel to be an incompleted task of life.

Two cases in point were recently presented by the author (1961) in another context. One is the life history of a healthy and average man, Bill Roberts, who as a traffic employee and later owner of a little shop, retired in his sixties and spent his later years in undisturbed good spirits and peace of mind.

Bill comes from a family of Kentucky farmers and small private and public employees. He married a high-school girl friend with whom he had four children and finds that his life was entirely satisfactory. His retirement at sixty-four followed a life that he essentially enjoyed and in which he accomplished what he was able to.

Also, now after his retirement, he finds enough worth-while things to do. Since his retirement, Bill has developed three main hobbies. He and his wife cultivate their little garden in which they raise beautiful roses and take care of

114

some fruit trees. He also does all the repair work and painting in his house and is proud of the good state in which he keeps all their appliances. As a third hobby, he has become the repairman for his grandchildren's toys and bicycles. This gives him a lot to do since he has nine grandchildren.

Bill calls his life happy and, if he used our terms, he would undoubtedly call it "fulfilled." He and his family lived what he calls a "decent and religious life without being fanatics." He says he had a good wife, and wonderful, healthy and normal children who gave them wonderful grandchildren. He has always been able to provide for his family. His life was thoroughly worthwhile to him, and he is lucky to have no major regrets. His one big decision to move to California proved to be a very good one.

Bill is essentially a very adaptive person who copes with given conditions as they are. He regretted, for example, that he did not have a better education, but he was compensated for that in informing and improving himself in ways accessible to him and he has no inferiority feelings about his status.

He has some degree of creative resourcefulness, which shows in the means with which he counteracted some of his misfortunes. As a boy of fourteen, he preferred making his own way to allowing an unloving stepfather to make him unhappy; again, he moved off to other parts of this country when his childhood family was dispersed; when his firm closed down, he used his bonus to take the family around the country before finding a new job; when his health weakened, he changed occupations.

It is this little creative resourcefulness that he was developing into his main old age hobby: A repairing for his home and his grandchildren. And it is characteristic of this man that his main hobby is an activity by means of which he is useful to his family. His life we might say, is to a great extent putting himself at the disposal of others.

His own need-satisfaction is not a dominating trend in him. Most significant here is the fact that after he had to relinquish the girl he loved, he decided to marry the girl who wanted him accepting what was offered and in a way considering her more than what his own desires had been.

He is a person to whom peace of mind is important. He gets his peace of mind in trying to please his family with whom he identifies strongly at all times, in doing what he thinks is right, and in living according to his faith (pp. 376-377).

The very creative life of one of our leading architects Richard Neutra was presented in the above mentioned volume as an example of a concept of human existence in which self-realization through creativity is of the essence. At sixty-eight, the feeling of undiminished ability and strength allow this master to go on working as if he were a youngster and in complete disregard of the fact that he had two serious heart attacks.

"Yes," he says if asked, "my coronaries; I have not time to think of them." Neutra feels that "to create, to work, to make people happy, that is what I am living for." He finds continuous pleasure in his work, in his contacts with people, his world-wide trips and, most important, in the unique marital oneness with his extraordinary wife Dione, his never failing companion and friend.

Bill Roberts and Richard Neutra represent examples of essentially successful and fulfilled lives.

With the term *fulfillment*, we refer to a closure experience that the person who lives with direction seems to be living toward. The experience of fulfillment does not occur only that once toward or at the end of life. There are momentary partial fulfillments of wishes, hopes, or expectations as long as we live. Gardner Murphy (1958) in discussing the concept of fulfillment, expresses the opinion that "there is no meaning in the conception of fulfilling human potentialities by rounding out a man and making him perfect, for he becomes qualitatively a new man as he grows" (p. 311). To me it seems, from my biographical evidence, that we do not lose nor discard, but that we accumulate and assemble fulfillments toward the end where life, for the person who sees his life as a whole, is as a whole experienced as fulfilled.

This total fulfillment aspect is of the essence for those who think of their existence as meant to represent an accomplishment; be it in their own eyes, in the eyes of their survivors, or in relationship to God or the Universe. They feel that their life was meant to bring certain values to materialization in this world and in themselves and that their fulfillment depends on whether they were essentially successful or not. These values may incorporate love and "happiness," health and the "good life," as Maslow (1959), for example, demonstrates in his self-realizing people—but the accent lies for these individuals on having contributed to the welfare and progress of others, possibly of mankind as a whole.

Those on the other hand, whose predominant tendency was toward "happiness," comfort, or security, or else toward inner harmony and peace, or toward a successful adjustment to given circumstances—these people who most likely represent the majority of mankind, are probably not living toward such a pronounced end result as the experience of fulfillment is. Yet they all, it seems, want to feel toward the end that they lived their life "right" or "successfully" or meaningfully and not "in vain."

I have repeatedly quoted the old woman in the Viennese old age home who, when interviewed about her life, concluded her autobiographical report with saying: "I am old and soon I shall be gone. I am poor and have nothing much to leave to anybody. I have no relatives left in the world. I am all alone. But I hope that after I am gone, some people will remember me kindly." This seems about all human beings can do and hope for, and the way this simple woman expressed it, seems to me truly human and an actually quite admirable outlook at the end of life.

Others expect a wider range or a deeper kind of after-effect of their lives. A teacher who answered one of my explorative questionnaires said that what she wanted was to feel that she had had some permanent effects on the children she had been teaching, in helping them to a future of success and happiness.

It seems to me from my own biographical as well as interview and questionnaire studies that *aftereffects* of their lives are important to many people. I found it surprising that in the considerable material that Orlans (1957) collected in England and that Feifel (1959) collected in several studies in this country very few references are made that seem to indicate concern with this problem of meaningful living and of aftereffects of one's life.

Feifel (1959) says that in response to the question "What does *death* mean to you?" he found two dominating outlooks.

One views death in a philosophic vein as the natural end process of life. The other is of a religious nature, perceiving death as the dissolution of bodily life and, in reality, the beginning of a new life. This finding, in a sense, broadly mirrors the interpretation of death in the history of Western thought. From these two opposite poles, Marcuse has suggested, two contrasting ethics may be derived. 'On the one hand the attitude toward death is the stoic or skeptic acceptance of the inevitable, or even the repression of the thought of death by life; on the other, the idealistic glorification of death is that which gives "meaning" to life, or is the precondition for the "true" life of man' (p. 117).

118

He gives examples of the two kinds of views of the very matter-of-fact outlook of people who resign themselves to death, because "you've lived your life," "you're at the end of your rope," "you've least to live for," and who, if they could do one more thing before death, would "travel all over the world" or something like that; and of the religious outlook of the person who would like to "give my belongings to charity," or "know more of God," and who hope for a life after death.

But his material does not give evidence of the "meaningful" death following a "meaningful" life as that ending toward which this individual has matured; the person who is "ripe" for his death and dies "his own death" as Rainer Maria Rilke put it. Death is then the fulfillment of life as, for example, Carl Jung (1934) sees it. "The negation of life's fulfillment" he says, "is synonymous with the refusal to accept the ending." And "Man can completely understand himself by integrating the death concept into his life." (p. 123)

Arnold Hutschnecker (1959) who contributed to Feifel's symposium, *The Meaning of Death,* clinical studies with dying patients, discusses specifically the relationship of fulfillment and death. He states: "It is disturbing to observe how few men and women have lived rich, full lives because of their emotional confusion and their difficulty in dealing effectively with the complexities of modern life" (p. 248). Yet he feels that "by and large, the man or woman who is about to die has made peace with himself." This means that toward the end, people seem to have a tendency to resign themselves to the limitations of their fulfillment. However, like Gardner Murphy in his evaluating discussion, I would be hesitant to generalize this statement.

Alexander and Adlerstein (1959) find, as we would expect, that nonreligious groups have greater anxieties related to death than religious groups. It would be interesting to know whether a subdivision of the nonreligious groups into those who find that they essentially fulfilled their goals of life as against those who consider their life to be essentially futile and a failure would make a difference or not.

Obviously, those who overcome the anxiety of death in committing *suicide* are more determined by their sense of failure than by their anxiety. Shneidman and Farberow (1957) find statements of guilt and self-blame besides expressions of hatred and vengeance to a higher degree in genuine than in simulated suicide notes. That means that the wish to die is most genuine in those who feel that their failure of life is a definite one. Self-destruction seems then the final resource of those who convinced themselves—rightly or wrongly—that they have no further possibility of any self-fulfillment.

4 *Values in Healthy aud*

Neurotic Development

1.
Value Problems and Value Conflicts

Value is an established preference on the grounds of selection. Values need not always be actual goals, but they always represent potential goals.

As potential goals, values may become problematic to an individual. One may ask himself whether a certain value is worth attaining, worth striving for, worth consideration.

Such a problem need not necessarily arise in terms of a conflict. But since an object or objective becomes a value by way of selection, it stands out from a background of others which may represent alternative choices. The alternative consideration may easily lead to a conflict.

A simple example may illustrate this point: Somebody

might consider attending a certain lecture. At first the question may simply be whether this attendance would be desirable. Then the plan may be seen in the light of an alternative, say of a restful evening spent at home; a conflict may then arise. What is the greater need of the moment? Then it may appear that there are duties involved, an obligation may be felt to attend the lecture, and so the question of desirability may in the end turn into a need-obligation conflict.

We will speak of *value problems* when the desirability of an object or objective is questioned. We will speak of *value conflicts* when alternative choices uphold a decision.

Since, from the beginning of life, the individual pursues his direction selectively, we can refer to this *selective activity* as the pursuit of factual values. Food preferences belong to the earliest psychosomatic self-expressions of the individual's selectivity.

Choice on the basis of comparison is observed first at about eight to ten months of age (as was shown in more detail in the last chapter). At this stage we notice that the child's look wanders back and forth between two toys offered to him simultaneously and he may then repeatedly reach for one after the other. A little later he may give evidence of an internal conflict among his own tendencies. He may reach and pull back and then reach for the other toy. In his verbal behavior, the one-and-a-half- to two-year-old child gives frequent evidence of *conflicting tendencies*. It may say "yes" and "no," one right after the other in answer to the same question, "do you like to play with this toy, to eat this vegetable," or anything else.

These conflicts in which the beginning ego tries to evaluate one's own needs and wishes are in a different category than the conflicts arising out of the *contradiction between the child's and the adult's goals.* The child's inner conflict between eating the forbidden candy and pleasing his mother through obedience has been considered by Freud as one of those basic conflict situations representing the nucleus of a neurotic development. This may take place if the child cannot resolve the conflict and responds with either repression of his desires or opposition against the mother.

Less attention has been paid to *unresolved need-conflicts* in which the individual cannot decide what he really wants now or what he wants more than anything else in the world. In fact, some people are unable to clarify for themselves what they truly want more than anything else in the world.

It is admittedly difficult to say to what degree some of those preferences that a person considers as ultimate actually represent his own nature. As we discussed before, from his very conception an individual develops so much in interaction with his environment that it becomes objectively impossible to discriminate the inborn and the acquired. Both are amalgamated from the start. Yet, as we also clarified, the individual is from the start selective in what he picks up and makes his own.

In view of this complexity of the developmental process, an individual's *value system* is very complex, not only as far as normative, but also as far as factual values are concerned. There are people who actually are unable to establish a clear *hierarchy of values* for themselves. This question comes up often in psychotherapy. "What do you *really* want the most for yourself?" or "What do you want more than anything else in the world?" a therapist may ask. And the patient may answer quite frequently, "I do not really know." Undoubtedly, the same "I don't know" would be the norm rather than the exception if asked of people in general.

There are at least two main factors that are responsible

for the excessive value problems and conflicts of our time. One is the enormous *range of choices* that our civilization and present-day Western culture offer in all areas of values. The modern department store with its immense array of available varieties of goods and luxuries offers perhaps the best example of the *embarras de richesse* to which the shopper of this time and age is exposed. The shopper's every need and wish, dreamed and even undreamed of possibilities of possession are anticipated in these products of modern industry. They lure the customer into a wonderland of goods that are offered to him with every suggestion possible. Thus the purchase of the shopper—and somehow we all seem to have become primarily *shoppers* in this modern world—is often determined by motives that are not really any more a matter of his current overt needs and desires, or his own objectives and goals. Even his most factual choices are more often than not a result of inculcation. It becomes a matter of personal strength, of pronounced dispositions, and of clear thinking to know what one really wants. No wonder that patients often say: "I do not seem to have a self, I really do not have the slightest idea who I am or what I want."

The anxiety that this situation arouses, is raised immensely with respect to normative and to group values, because a threat of condemnation is attached to the wrong choices in these areas. Condemnation by whom? By relatives and friends, by society and its representatives, by God and the churches, and by who knows whom else. The reasons for this status quo are well known and have often been discussed. They lie in the nearly complete *dissolution of and disillusion in* the previously existing value systems. This, then, is the second reason for the increased value problems of our time. There is no belief, no conviction that has not been

124

attacked, doubted, or shattered by just as good arguments as have helped to uphold it.

This places the average person before choices that he is not fully equipped to make. He would often much rather have somebody tell him what beliefs to adhere to than make decisions himself. He just does not know which arguments, which criteria are the best.

Then value problems and value conflicts in our time are very often due not to neurotic indecision but to valid reasons of incompetence to make these decisions. Therefore the question: *what makes indecision neurotic?* becomes a much more pertinent question in our time than it ever was before. In view of the existing complexities of modern life, decisiveness may at times be more the result of neurotic motives than indecision, since indecision may at times reflect the status of uncertainty of the cultural value system. Tolerance of ambiguity may at times, as has been shown, be a sign of greater strength. (E. Frenkel, 1948, 1949.)

This means that in our time and culture the inability to resolve value conflicts is not only, perhaps not even primarily, due to an inability to accept the frustrations, the limitations, that society and reality impose on the individual. But nearly as often we may find an individual in unresolvable conflict because he has need-conflicts or lacks a clear direction of his own so that he cannot decide between possible choices that a fluctuating cultural value system seems to permit.

A case in point may be presented and may also prepare for our later discussion of the therapist's role.

Georgia, a woman of thirty-three, married, without children, has a seventy-year-old ailing mother who has been living with Georgia much of the eight years of her marriage. Georgia's husband has forever been objecting to this situation, as he felt the demanding, petulant, constantly complaining old woman disturbed the peace of their home, came between him and his wife, and dominated his wife unbearably. In fact, these disagreeable qualities of hers were the main reason that none of the other two children ever wanted to keep their mother for any length of time in their homes and had lately even detached themselves entirely from her and from any obligations to her.

When the couple felt they could not resolve their problem without help, and when the husband threatened to leave because he felt his wife cared more for her mother than for him, Georgia agreed finally to enter psychotherapy, as she had to admit she was unduly under the influence of her mother.

The problem was a double one. First, there was undoubtedly the situation of a neurotic dependency that Georgia had developed in her relationship with her mother. Second there was the problem of right and wrong in dealing with the situation of a very sick old mother who did not have the means to take care of herself.

The therapist suggested that the patient defer her decisions regarding her mother's fate till she had a clearer understanding of her relationship with her mother and of her own emotional involvement in the matter.

During less than two years of psychotherapy, Georgia was gradually able to detach herself from this mother who had dominated her whole life, who had compensated for her own marital failure with what she considered a complete devotion to her children, particularly to this youngest daughter with whom she early established an extremely close relationship. Georgia, a soft-spoken, gentle, and rather weak personality had developed an extreme dependency, as well as an excessive feeling of obligation toward her mother and was consequently also quite unable to grow into a healthy sex relationship with her husband. When Georgia was able to face the problem of standing up to her mother for the sake of saving her marriage and her own independence, she was confronted with the second problem, which we consider of a different nature than the problem of her neurotic dependency.

This was the problem of evaluating her right to live her own life as against the duty to take care of a mother, whose life seemed actually endangered and whose condition was aggravated by severe psychosomatic sufferings whenever she was threatened with separation from her daughter.

Georgia and her husband decided that it was their duty to set up the mother as comfortably as was possible in her own home town with some household help for which they made considerable sacrifices. They took the risk of contributing to an aggravation of her condition and they weathered her scorn. But they felt they had no other choice.

The case in question required a decision about values that in another culture and even half a century ago in our culture might have been quite a different one. Our time and culture would be inclined to give the young couple the right to their own happiness regardless of the undoubtedly maladjusted older woman's unhappiness. But even in our time, some people might feel that this case is controversial. Georgia, anyway, had to stand up to several relatives who took it upon themselves to remind her of her duties toward her mother.

The problem of how to take care of this mother must thus be considered one dependent on cultural standards, while the dependency relationship must be considered a neurotic problem. Thus a neurotic and a value problem must be discriminated in this case.

What is the therapist's role in the handling of this type of conflict? There are, obviously, no absolutely binding rules in existence, except that most therapists at the present time would wish the patient to work out this problem as much as possible by herself.

The patient in question entered therapy under the assumption that she would get advice as to what to do with her mother as well as with her marriage. The therapist told her that after some time, she would probably find her own answer to those problems. Furthermore, the patient who had several psychosomatic complaints, was willing to defer any decisions she might have to make till she got a better understanding of herself and her relationship with her mother.

The therapist's conviction that in the existing situation actually two different problems were involved, was not brought out till very much later as the patient was emotionally much too involved to see anything clearly. Later, it was mostly with the help of a therapy group in which Georgia participated during her second year that she was made aware of the double nature of her problems.

When finally the *cultural value problem of duty toward the mother* as against the *right to one's own life* was brought out, the therapist took the stand that different people and different times might solve this problem differently and that the patient had to find her own solution. When asked about her stand in this matter, the therapist said that she herself felt everyone had the right and the duty to live his own life and then do as well as possible by others.

This then is an example of the therapist's willingness to explain her own position in the matter of a nonresolved cultural value problem, furthermore it is an example of the therapist's inducing clarification of this versus the neurotic dependency problem.

It is also an example of normal versus neurotic value problems and conflicts. The example was chosen as one that might not be too controversial, because the changes of cultural value aspects and the problems that they imply for everyone might be generally acknowledged. But there are other conflicts in which this might not be equally clear and therefore it will be necessary to introduce a criterion for the distinction of normal and of neurotic value problems and conflicts. This is particularly necessary if and inasmuch as we feel the therapist might be entitled or required to take a stand in the one, but not in the other respect.

2.

Value Conflicts and Healthy Development

The psychotherapist is usually faced with a neurotic value development in his patient. Its restructuring is part of the accomplishment expected from him. But how does he conceive of healthy versus neurotic values?

Within the still unsettled question of the definition of mental health—see Fritz C. Redlich's (1957) and Marie Jahoda's (1958) extensive surveys—the problem of what healthy values are is perhaps the most intricate.

The reason lies in the great divergence of opinions about the nature, the origin, and the role of values.

An individual's opposition, for example, to some value that ranks high in his environment, may be judged differently by those who believe in an essentially social origin and role of all values as compared with those who believe in an "unfolding" of the self and in self-realization.

An example in point is found in the interesting study, "Neurotic Patterns in the Family," presented by E. J. Cleveland and W. D. Longaker (1957). These authors interpret

129

the neurotic solutions of value conflicts in the development of the group members whom they study exclusively in terms of cultural determinants. To start with, they establish in this group a "cultural value configuration" with "incompatible orientations." Then they see the "individual development and personality integration" impaired by a "culturally recurrent mode of self-devaluation."

Thus when they describe the rebellion of one family member, Alice Mary, who "added something of her own," this something of her own was only that she wanted to be "different" from her parents. Her phantasies of a feminine role, her phantasies in connection with her "desire for a stable existence close to nature, renunciation of economic and social ambition, together with more enjoyment of love, sharing, and interpersonal vivacity" (p. 187) are not given credit as tendencies to a creative expansion that Alice Mary, under the pressure of the given circumstances, is not able to bring to materialization. Instead they are seen exclusively as evidence of her opposition. This is explained by her mother's rejection. However, rebellion against rejection and tendencies to be "different" could assume more destructive or more incoherent forms than these phantasies indicate. In other words, these phantasies seem to be evidence of constructive and creative tendencies of this personality.

The authors themselves seem to question at some point the validity of their assumptions. "Does neurosis," they ask (p. 188), "sometimes occur with no, or a very slight background of cultural conflict? For example, does organ inferiority, bodily illness, or disaster sometimes play the most critical part in the development of neurosis?"

How strangely remote is this point of view from the assumption of internally conflicting dispositions! An assumption such as Karen Horney's, for example, of the origin of value conflicts in mutually contradictory goals within the personality, seems to represent an opposite extreme.

The author feels that a theory is needed in which both the environmental impact as well as the individual's own tendencies find equal consideration. The previously briefly introduced theory of four basic tendencies of life offers these possibilities. The assumption was that the tendencies toward need satisfaction, toward self-limiting adaptation, toward expansive creativity, and toward the upholding of the internal order are primary and present at all times in an individually as well as developmentally varying distribution.

From this theory, it becomes understandable that the more adaptive individual is more exposed to the environmental impact, while the more creative individual remains more selective and is more preoccupied with his own strivings. His conflicts are more apt to originate in his own contradictory or incompatible disposition, while the adaptive individual's problems result primarily from his responsiveness to environmental pressures and demands. It also seems evident that for the more adaptive individual's internal order it is of paramount importance that he comes to terms with his environment, while the more creative individual's internal order depends more on what he can do with himself under any given circumstances.

A healthy or a neurotic value development must depend thus both on the individual's ability to integrate his own strivings and on his ability to cope with the environmental impacts.

Two cases with some comparable characteristics will be presented very briefly to demonstrate the different handling of value conflicts in the development of two women.

Linda,[1] now fifty-three years old, wife of a journalist, mother of a twenty-year-old daughter who goes to college, grew up on Southern California ranches, which were managed by her father. She is the oldest of a family of five, and from an early age was her mother's helper with the younger siblings and the household. She always was and still is very close to her gay and loving mother. This mother was, in spite of the burden of her big household, which she had to run with rather limited means, a very tolerant, easy-going woman. She stood up for her children to the father who was apt to be a disciplinarian and to live by principles.

The family was of English and Scottish background, Presbyterians on the one side, Mormons on the other side, fairly but not exaggeratedly religious and with a rather simple, middle-class outlook on life. There were few intellectual interests and it was one of Linda's early conflicts that she became greatly interested in books and study, which her father declared nonsense for a woman.

When at fourteen she announced that she wanted to go to college and later study medicine, she ran into serious opposition from her father who felt that women belonged in the house and that she should marry and have children. He also pointed out to her that their economic circumstances were such that they could absolutely not afford having her go to college. Linda's teachers on the other hand encouraged the highly intelligent girl to try to pursue her studies. Thus, she took college preparatory work in high school hoping her father might later approve of her going on to college and hoping ways and means might be found to realize her dream.

In trying to analyze her feelings toward her father at this point, Linda says that she resented his narrowmindedness, but that she never harbored very bitter feelings against him. She calls herself a realist in acknowledging the financial plight of her family. She also calls herself an optimist who

---

1. This case was discussed also in the previous chapter in another context.

believed some way or other would open up for her as it actually later did.

Her own motives also were not completely undivided. In using our terminology, we might say that Linda was always somewhat split between her adaptive and her creative tendencies.

Her striving toward creative expansion resulted from a strong intellectual curiosity and urge to get from science more enlightenment about life and the universe than the churches of her parents seemed to provide for her. There was also the motive of having a career of her own and being as free to pursue it as men seemed to be. Finally, she liked the idea of doing a service for people, but one based on a good education.

On the side of her tendencies to adaptive self-limitation, she experienced as a strong motive her love for her mother and her younger siblings, whose mother substitute she liked to play. Also, she did not dislike household work and she felt their big family was fun to be with.

When, however, at nineteen an uncle and aunt suggested she come to Honolulu to stay with them if she could find herself a job, she defied her father and went.

While there, she met after a year, her future husband, who favored her college education. Linda felt that this combination of marriage and home, college education and a career of her own with later planned motherhood would bring her complete fulfillment.

This was actually more or less the case except for a period of marital troubles, which also delayed her child's birth to some degree. She continued for some years to feel the conflict between the tendencies to dedicate herself to her housewifely duties and to those of a career woman, but eventually she managed to combine both successfully.

Why can we call this development essentially free of neurotic predicaments, even though we might acknowledge a slight neurotic involvement in this dichotomy of basic tendencies? In order to determine this, we will have to decide on some *criteria* for what we want to call neurotic. This decision is nearly as difficult as the decision regarding criteria for mental health, as the previously mentioned recent surveys demonstrated.

3.
Value Conflicts and Neurotic Development

Many different criteria for the definition of neurotic behavior and the neurotic process are proposed by many authors. In view of the fact that no unanimity has been reached, every new writer has to make up his own mind as to which definition seems the most acceptable to him.

Decisive conditions for the development of the neurotic process seem to the author, with slight alterations from Kubie to be: firstly, the existence of *psychological tensions* due to frustrations or conflicts with which the individual cannot cope; secondly, the generating of *repressions* of those processes resulting from these unacceptable frustrations and unresolvable conflicts; thirdly, the production of *substitutive* solutions of a symbolic character.

This sequence of events leads then to that *inflexibility* or *unalterability* which Lawrence Kubie (1957, p. 81) points out as the essence of the neurotic process. Rollo May (1953) calls it, the individual's "inability to act as an autonomous self."

The decisive cause for the neurotic's inflexibility, which prevents his freedom of choice, his adequate perception and mastery of reality, his integration, and most of all his inner development, is seen by Kubie to be faulty and obviously un-

134

changeable *interpretation*, due to distorted symbolic thinking.

Kubie's answer to "the question of what forces determine the evolution of this neurotic process" is that "many variables determine this—e.g., physiological, cultural, and social forces, individual idiosyncratic events, catastrophic early experiences, and early but continuous stresses" (p. 85).

Kubie's careful formulation allows for congenital as well as environmental factors to become codeterminants in the development of neurosis. However, the question of how both come into effect seems so far still largely unanswered.

An earlier definition of Alexander and French (1946) gives a sort of a key formula. They say:

> Psychoneurosis is a failure of the individual to deal successfully with a given situation, a failure to find socially acceptable gratification for subjective needs under given circumstances. This failure depends upon the balance between the ego's adaptability and the difficulty of the confronting problem. When the situation demands greater powers of integration than the ego possesses a neurosis develops. Whether the ego became incapacitated in childhood, adolescence, or adult life, and how it is limited by constitutional endowment, are secondary questions. According to this concept of the causation of neurosis, both unfavorable constitutional endowment and infantile experiences on the one hand, and traumatic experiences of later life on the other, must be taken into consideration (p. 8).

In this definition, the difficulty of the given situation is weighed against a number of given factors in the individual. Named are, "the ego's adaptability," "powers of integration," "incapacitation."

What impresses in this as well as in some of the other enumerations of factors as, for example, reported by Jahoda (1958) and by Redlich (1957) is that they are not really

135

derived in a systematic way and that we do not yet seem to have a systematic approach to the problem of the different factors that may determine forms of adjustment.

In the foregoing chapter we showed that from child psychological observations a primary disposition to be more active and expansive or to be more passive and self-limiting can be distinguished. It was reasoned that the more active and expansive individual would be better able to pursue the satisfaction of his needs and/or to become creative in his environment. It also was concluded that the more passive and self-limiting individual would be more disposed to hold up his own internal order and/or to fit himself adaptively into his environment. The theory of four basic tendencies had been previously hypothesized on a theoretical basis and seemed to fit well with child psychological data.

It is assumed that while in all human beings these four tendencies are at all times in operation, they determine the individual's actions in varying degrees. Motivation as well as experience influence the predominance pattern of these tendencies.

The theory of the four tendencies offers a basis for a systematic approach to the problem of different adjustment patterns.

The more aggressively need-satisfying and creatively expansive person might find adjustment easier as long as he is not opposed and obstructed to the degree that he is stymied. The more passively self-limiting and order-upholding individual may adjust more easily as long as his hypersensitivity is not hurt and as long as he feels fully accepted.

There may be equilibrium or conflict and disequilibrium among these tendencies and there may be integration and direction or lack of integration and lack of direction in their functioning.[2]

These internal conflicts of basic tendencies as well as their poor integration and the underlying pronounced onesidedness of tendencies predispose the individual in the author's opinion to the development of neuroses even if circumstances are not absolutely unfavorable.

The impact of unfavorable circumstances adds to the difficulties in which the one-sided and internally conflicted individual is apt to get involved.

In the previously discussed case of Linda, a neurotic development is avoided in spite of considerable environmental pressure. Linda's father demands that she gives up the pursuit of interests that are important to her. Perhaps, if the pressure had been still greater than it was, if, for example, her mother, too, had forbidden Linda to read and to take academic subjects in school, then she might not have been able to cope with the imposed frustrations.

On the other hand, Linda impresses us with her ability to tolerate tension and to bide her time. She showed this ability again later in life, when due to career problems of her husband and a long illness of her daughter, she had once more to defer her own study interests. She devoted herself for several years entirely to her family, and it was only in her forties that she was able to return to school. She was capable of generating renewed enthusiasm and she had enough elasticity and energy to earn her degree at this late date and to enter her chosen profession.

2. Unfortunately, we do not yet possess techniques with which to measure equilibrium or integration. Thus far they are only estimated with the help of clinical judgment and experience.

Thus it would seem as if Linda were possessed of a combination of adaptive and creative tendencies that allowed her to preserve her integrity and inner freedom of action under adverse as well as under favorable influences. She seems able to resolve her conflicts and to find constructive solutions.

Even at times when she finds it hard to cope with the given situation, she *does not try to repress* any of her problems and conflicts. She acknowledges them for what they are and resolves them on a temporary basis, deferring final decisions for later.

Her *interpretations* are all extremely positive. She feels sure of her mother's love even though the mother cannot pay her much attention. She hopes to find ways and means to convince her father or anyway to make her studies possible at some later time and she prepares for that as well as she can without getting into an actual fight with her father. The moment she sees an opportunity and she feels she has submitted long enough, she acts independently, and she uses good judgment with respect to the timing of this step.

Her own conflicting motives were gradually *integrated* to her satisfaction after a period of doubt and struggle. Thus, in spite of deprivations, a cultural climate that was not favorable to her best self-realization, and inner value conflicts, Linda succeeded ultimately in setting up values and goals toward a true fulfillment.

Since it so happens that in the author's case material there is the example of a very neurotic value development under comparable circumstances, it seems useful to make this comparative study.

Barbara was a young girl, twenty-nine-years old when she came into psychotherapy in a state near breakdown. Her problem was that she had lost confidence and hope, because the things she had lived for and believed in had not turned out as she had hoped they would. She felt she was a failure, and was at a complete loss regarding everything. This "everything" included not only her own present and future life but also the understanding of what had happened in the past and why it could happen.

Barbara also grew up as the oldest daughter of a large family and like Linda, she became a substitute mother for her siblings. But different from Linda, she apparently did not feel sure of her mother's love for her, although it took her several months of psychotherapy before she could admit this disappointment to herself.

The reasons for her basic insecurity in her relationship with her mother seem to have been that her mother fell ill soon after Barbara was born and that, before she could devote much time and attention to her first child, a second child was born. It seems that from then on the mother always appealed to Barbara to help her with the new babies and Barbara felt that helping her mother was the only way in which she could get her mother's affection for herself.

She tried to convince herself that this was as it should be and this conviction was strongly enhanced by her Catholic upbringing. Her parents interpreted and taught their children their religion as a very strict philosophy of life according to which nobody was entitled to ask things for himself, but everybody was expected to help and serve others, particularly the family.

During the first psychotherapy months when the therapist asked Barbara what she really wanted for herself out of life, the girl's automatic answer was that she did not want anything for herself at all, in fact she did not even care what happened to her. She believed firmly that her life was valuable only to the degree to which she dedicated it to others. Since she loved pretty clothes and all sorts of good things, and since above all she craved sex, she felt very badly about herself and very depressed regarding what she thought was expected from her.

Yet it never occurred to her to doubt her religion or her

parent's interpretation of it. She felt they were right, she identified fully with these concepts and asked from herself complete submission to the rules as she understood them.

Barbara was, like Linda, a very intelligent girl and had hoped to go to college. She was also encouraged by her teachers. But due to her father's poor earning capacity—he was a construction worker and often without a job—there was absolutely no money for her or any of the children's future education available, and she was needed by the family. Thus, unlike Linda, she resigned herself without reservation and hope to taking a job instead of going to college, because, unlike Linda, she accepted without opposition, her father's ruling in this matter and also because she did not feel as strong an urge for an intellectual development of her own and for creative work as did Linda.

Her disappointment became extreme when finally after many years of sacrifice she felt that everything was in vain. The reasons for this feeling of futility were that she had not been able to prevent the family from falling apart nor to help her younger siblings to a somewhat adequate home life. What happened was that her mother became very ill and died without having given Barbara the feeling that she acknowledged sufficiently what the girl had tried to do. Furthermore, the father took to excessive drinking and was less amenable than ever. The other children went off into jobs and marriages without indicating the feelings of closeness and gratitude that Barbara believed to have earned from them.

So what was the use of having believed in what she did if it proved to bring no rewards at all. Yet she could not get herself to surrender any of her beliefs because she felt that they gave her self-esteem, they represented her whole identity.

In establishing the neurotic trends of this case in comparison with Linda's healthy pattern, we must first of all point to the *inflexibility* with which Barbara was clinging to all her convictions without ever modifying any part of them.

To start with, her religion would not have forbidden her

to try to get enjoyment out of life for herself. Since she was intelligent and had the benefit of a much better education than her parents, she could have, like Linda, after some thinking of her own, come to the conclusion that her parent's interpretation of their religion was one-sided and extreme.

But Barbara was unable to free herself to this degree from her parent's ideas because she felt she could have their affection and recognition only if she complied as fully as she did with their wishes. This was her interpretation of her relationship with them, which she later had to recognize as faulty. It appeared later that all her serving the family did not help her one bit to being more loved or as much praised as she would have liked to be.

What was responsible for these *wrong interpretations?* Two things seem to stand out. One is that Barbara was much more *sensitive* to her mother's not paying her attention as a young child than Linda was. She did not feel loved, she felt disregarded. The other is that Barbara had a much more one-sided and extreme tendency to *adapt* herself to all her given circumstances than Linda who made her mental reservations when obeying her father and who kept her tendencies to creative expansion intact and ready to take over in due time. Barbara repressed her disappointment and tried to earn what seemed denied to her.

While with these observations we point out mostly Barbara's own weaknesses, we must not forget to mention that another suppressive factor was given in the exceedingly strong impact of the *cultural value system impressed on her.* The actual severity of the dictates of the religion to which the family was committed, represented a stronger cultural value pressure than Linda's.

Summarizing the comparison of the two cases, we can

141

say that Linda's better adjustment was due to her own lesser vulnerability, to her less exclusively adaptive and more creative trends, which made her more independent and more resourceful and allowed her to interpret her situation more favorably. Furthermore, it was due also to the less rigorous impact of the cultural value system to which she was exposed.

What is the role of the psychotherapist in a case like Barbara's?

This case has, so it seems to the author, two very different aspects: one is that of a *neurotic value development*, the other is that of a *religious value system*.

As far as the neurotic value development is concerned, the therapist will find no particular problem in the procedure. He will see his obvious goal in helping this girl to a proper self-understanding of her relationship with her parents. He will help her to become aware of how her subjective and possibly faulty interpretations, such as that her mother could love her only if she deserved and earned this love; that she had to play the role of complete self-sacrifice for the family; that her religion demanded all this from her, and so on. He will help her to see that if she took all these things upon herself, differently from all other children of the family, she wanted perhaps not just to hold the family together, but to excel everybody else in the family, and so on.

He will furthermore try to let her recognize similar trends of perfectionism in her present behavior, in which again she wants to prove herself as a shining example to her Church and to God.

But after all this has been sufficiently worked through there still remains the problem of certain rules set up by her religion, or by society, by which Barbara wants to abide.

142

The position of the psychotherapist in this type of value problem was debated by the previously mentioned Los Angeles Study Group on Values.

Several therapists had cases that were comparable to that of Barbara. Examples were quoted in which birth control, premarital or extramarital intercourse, or divorce were brought up by patients whose religion or ethical convictions forbade these actions.

Three views were expressed by different discussants. One opinion was that in the course of therapy the patient should overcome what some therapists considered false superego principles; the second was that a patient like Barbara should be made to recognize that the degree of her sex needs might be neurotic; the third, also the author's view, was that if these needs existed, but if strict adherence to her beliefs guaranteed her the integrity of her personality, she had to accept and cope with her frustration.

Not only with her frustration, but in fact also with her *guilt* feelings. The necessity of experiencing a degree of guilt feelings by a person who abides by standards of any kind, is of course again a matter of debate.

This, it was agreed, might be unfavorable for her health. However, the assumption of *health being the highest value,* was recognized as not necessarily valid, but as debatable. It was mentioned before that this was pointed out by analysts as early as the twenties, and it has been emphasized since then repeatedly.

However, the grounds on which an individual's choice and decision should be made and accepted as right for him, have not exactly been clarified.

A corroboration of the author's point of view that conflicts of values and preferences are normal and should be accepted and coped with, is found in a recent study by Morris, Eiduson, and O'Donovan (1960).

The authors used preference ratings on thirteen possible "ways to live," which Morris (1956) had previously worked out and studied with a sample of college students in a number of cultures. The "ways" were rated now by patients of the Clinic of the Hacker Foundation for Psychiatric Research and Education, as well as by a control group.

Among the interesting results, the following statements confirm our thinking.

> The data do show evidence linking the degree of severity of the disturbance with the amount of conflict among the values held by the disturbed person. It does not follow that conflicts among values necessarily lead to difficulties which call for psychotherapy—for many persons without such disturbances have as many, or more, value conflicts as do the patients. For one reason or other, the patient is unable to find efficient ways of managing such conflicts, which thereby become anxiety producing and incapacitating.
>
> It seems rather as if the "pathic" ways to live are distorted, inefficient, and hence unsatisfying versions of the same ways to live found in healthy persons. Psychotherapy, for quite independent reasons, aims at what this suggests: not the changing of the values of the disturbed person but helping him develop more effective techniques of realizing those values he holds (p. 31).

This is exactly what was done in the case of Barbara. Gradually, in the course of considerable time, Barbara learned to accept her needs as being partially in conflict with her religious convictions. Like other persons in this situation, she found a compromise in occasionally giving in to her needs while at other times upholding her beliefs.

144

The worthlessness of her existence without the previous dedication to a cause and the lack of interest in her own future she learned gradually to overcome in giving herself a new goal. She began devoting her free time to her college education. This goal still linked her partly to her mother who had always talked admiringly of the values of a good education. On the other hand, this goal and image of education related her to her therapist, in whom she had found to a degree a mother substitute.

The choice of this goal was a good one, because Barbara could still feel herself loyal to the memory of her mother. But her tie-up with her mother was no longer the pathological yearning for a love she had not received.

Barbara did not require the therapist's help in the way in which Georgia needed assistance for the solution of her conflict. Barbara kept her values and her value conflicts and she took it upon herself to cope with them. She also found her own new goal. Even though her struggle was hard and her life for the time being not happy, she was able to pull out of her neurotic breakdown and to open herself a way to a new freedom.

5 The Role of Values and Beliefs in Human Life

1.
Value, Meaning, and Fulfillment

Even the people who are free to choose their values and goals, may have problems and conflicts due to the complexities of our inner and outer conditions of life. The outer conditions provide pressures and sometimes too many choices. The inner conditions consist in a multiplicity of sometimes conflicting tendencies. To this comes modern man's doubt in the validity of our beliefs regarding chosen goals and values. Let us ask first, what are the healthy person's guiding considerations in making choices? Is there any decisive motive or is there always an interplay of many?

In looking back at the case of Linda, which was presented as an example of a relatively healthy development, we find an interplay of a number of conflicting tendencies. Linda wants to please her parents and help her mother, but Linda wants also to satisfy her mental curiosity and her intellectual ambition. She wants to study and eventually to enter a profession where she can help people. Simultaneously with this, she also pursues other goals: to make her marriage a successful one and to be a good mother to her child. There is at most times of her life a balance between the four basic tendencies, with an alternating prevalence between adaptive self-limitation and creative expansion.

The two main values between which she fluctuated, belonging and dedicating herself to family life on the one hand, and her professional development and success on the other hand were to some degree conflicting. But on the whole, Linda struck a happy balance between both and seemed to be able to cope with a certain amount of tension that always existed.

Why did Linda select and concentrate on just those two specific goals?

When the question was put to her whether she ever had cared for becoming very wealthy, having the opportunity to buy herself all she wanted, to travel, to have lots of fun or else to be outstanding, well known, a person of influence in the community or really famous, she said: All these things sounded very nice, but had never been important to her, in fact, she felt, if she had had these possibilities opened to her, she might have felt at a loss, not knowing what to do with it all; it might have bewildered her; she could not have concentrated on the things that she really wanted to do.

And why did she want to do these things rather than the other things?

These, she said, made her happy, they were meaningful to her, this other "stuff" did not really mean anything to her.

And what did she mean by "meaningful"?

"These things, my professional work for and with people, my understanding of them and my life for and with my family, in these things I grow and develop, this is really *me* in all this and with this I am working in the right direction toward some final satisfaction."

What Linda says in this part of the interview is that she selected certain things with which she could most fully *identify,* this made them *meaningful,* they allowed her to *develop* and they promised *fulfillment.*

We might ask why could she identify just with the things she selected and not with other goals. In her own words it is because she feels, "this is really *me.*" That means, that these things *are* identical with her, she does not have to *develop* an identity. This could mean that they actually grow out of her as her own talents and her own inclinations. Partly, it may mean that long ago she established an identity with them, in incorporating her mother's dedicated love for example.

Since these things *are* herself, she can feel that their growth is her own. And since she realizes herself in them, they will bring her fulfillment.

Barbara primarily valued, during the first part of her therapy two rather opposite things that she constantly strove to reconcile in herself. She wanted very much to find a man who would give her besides full sex satisfaction, beautiful clothes, a comfortable life, and sensitive understanding. On the other hand, she felt that her worthiness as a human being was given to her by her religion and her Church, with which she felt completely identified.

When asked, how could it be explained that after her previous complete dedication to her family she was now so desirous of those other things, she said she had exhausted

148

herself, she felt empty and deprived, she had not gotten anything back in return for what she gave. Now she felt she had to get something for herself, then maybe later she would again be able to dedicate herself to a man who gave her love.

Obviously, Barbara had experienced such a deep need-frustration that starved as she was, satisfaction of needs was of the essence. it actually seemed a condition of her further development, but the situation looked for a while rather hopeless in view of the strings attached to the condition. The strings attached came from Barbara's religious convictions, the main thing in her life representing her identity.

This identity she carried with her from her parents and the cultural matrix of her childhood, while her cravings were all her own. They distinguished her completely from the rest of the family, from her sisters and brothers, none of whom ever expressed similar desires or ambitions.

But Barbara felt these things would "mean much" to her, because she never had them, and they were what she longed for.

Of course, her siblings did not have them and Linda, for that matter, did not have them either. If Barbara wanted them so much and they "meant" so much to her, this might have been due to the fact that her frustrations were greater than those of the others or that she just had a greater natural craving for such things.

Be that as it may, the point we want to make is that all these values are obviously *assigned* to objects that the individual endows with meaning.

This is essentially also the concept of the existential psychology, that an existence is chosen and a meaning assigned. The idea is that the choice should be made in the direction of the individual's *best potentials*. We have demonstrated in two other places (1960, 1961) with examples that in many, if not most cases it is not easy at all to determine this best potential in advance. A person might easily find out that although he had conscientiously and responsibly searched he made a "wrong" choice. "Wrong" for him could mean that he does not believe any more in what he was so eagerly striving for, or that failure makes him realize this was not what he should have attempted.

Two examples of "wrong" self-destinations for individuals, even though in themselves meaningful and valuable goals of life were given in the first edition of this author's (1933) book *The Human Course of Life*. They were the self-sacrifices of the Polish patriot Mochnacki and the French Jesuit Father Paul Ginhac.

Mochnacki was an idealistic young man who tried at the beginning of the last century to free Poland from the Russian sovereignty. Although well educated and assisted by an equally idealistic group of young patriots, his attempt failed miserably because it was ill prepared and quickly discovered; not only was it completely suppressed, but it also brought Mochnacki deep shame and despair because during his imprisonment, under tortures he betrayed all secrets.

This man attempted something for which he was not equipped and which perhaps no one would have been able to accomplish.

The French Jesuit Father Paul Ginhac, on the other hand, was obviously well equipped to serve his church in those offices to which he was assigned. But to him, a vigorous peasant youth who had been dedicated to the church by his family, the disciplined and closed-in life of the monastery was a continuous torture. For a long time he rebelled and tried to get out of a life that he felt was not his and not for him. But the tears of his mother and the convincing words

150

of an educated priest led him to take his final vows as a priest.

Some of his sayings reveal the despair of a man, who while as a teacher and priest did fulfill a great potential in an exemplary way yet felt during all his life, that this life was not for him. "One has to condemn oneself once to death and then carry out this sentence every day," he said in his thirties. When he was fifty-three: "My way is difficult and usually I am deprived of all enlightenment and consolation." He believed that self-castigation would help him. But he still suffered in "loneliness" and "darkness."

Although it was decided upon as something he believed in as the worthiest cause, and although carried out so well that Father Ginhac enjoyed the highest esteem of his church and of everybody who worked with him, his chosen self-dedication did not render any feeling of satisfaction to this man.[1]

We might complete the list of these biographical references with one more example of thwarted dedication, the story of the famous obstetrician Ignaz Semmelweis. As is generally known, in the middle of the last century this great

---

1. The psychologist might very readily suspect that this man's suffering was not quite as genuine as all that, but that perhaps he obtained masochistic pleasures of which he was not aware.

The data of this biography that was available to me, is not sufficient enough in the analytic sense to substantiate or to invalidate this assumption. Personally, I gained the impression of sincerity.

But the point is not really whether such factors come into play or not. What matters is that the destination given this man was "wrong" in terms of a healthy self-fulfillment or a healthy fulfillment of potentialities.

The situation is a little different in the following case of Ignaz Semmelweis. His task was obviously "right" for him inasmuch as he brought out his best abilities in the right occupation. But again, for the strength this man had available, his suffering was too much, the sacrifice too great to call this a successful fulfillment of potentialities. Assuming he was fulfilling self-punishment needs, or satisfaction of injustice-collecting, the result was a complete collapse, which ruined the man.

Hungarian physician discovered that puerperal fever, which had killed so many new mothers, was actually contracted in the hospital. He experimented successfully with various new techniques of disinfection of the obstetricians' hands and instruments.

Instead of recognition, Semmelweis was met with ridicule and opposition. When about twenty years later his techniques of hygiene finally began to be accepted, Semmelweis was bitter and tired from his fighting; he developed a psychosis and died soon after.

This case represents a third variety of "wrong" self-destination. This man did what was "right" for him in every sense. Not only was he a warmhearted and humane person who was deeply affected by the tragedy of so many young mothers' dying because of what he recognized as some maltreatment, but he was also well equipped to solve the problem ingeniously and comprehensibly. Yet an adequate success was denied to him due to unfavorable external circumstances that he did not know how to combat. Still in this case, there is a greater inner fulfillment because Semmelweis knew his was the future, if not the present and his findings were correct and valuable.

These three stories even though pertaining to the lives of unusual men, should suffice to illustrate our point that the choice of the "right" goals and values is difficult and complicated. A choice might be "right" under one aspect and not "right" under another. Neither the individuals' potentialities nor those of the external circumstances are forseeable.

Examples such as these present real problems for the self-realization theory: first of all, the best potential may not

152

be always clear and, secondly, realizing the best potential may not always prove to be successful in terms of subjective fulfillment. They are also a problem for those existentialists who like V. E. Frankl (1957) make the individual responsible for finding his "specific task." He admits that it is not only the neurotics who have difficulty doing this.

The "right" task in Frankl's sense is not necessarily one that leads to self-realization; in fact he emphasizes that this is no goal at all. But as we could see in the case of Father Ginhac, the greatest, and in the eyes of others most successful and valuable, dedication did not give him any sense of satisfaction, because it was not right for him, since it thwarted forever some of his most vital needs.

Thus, it seems to me, we cannot rule out the individual's needs and their actualization.

Instead it seems to be true—we saw it in the case of Linda—that we find our most complete fulfillment if we can be ourselves and do what we like to do while dedicating ourselves to a task we believe in. In this we transcend ourselves, but simultaneously we also satisfy ourselves. One without the other throws us off balance. Not even this most dedicated priest to whom we referred before, was able to reach peace of mind.

In conclusion I must state that in my opinion the finding of our "life task" (V. E. Frankl, 1957), if there is such a thing, is extremely difficult. In fact, because of the innumerable counteractive circumstances of life, it is the rare person who is able to designate the appropriate task for himself and who then is also able to carry it through.

This latter problem will lead us now to new and further considerations.

2.
Value and Identity

The concept of identity, which Erik Erikson (1959) derived from Freud and which he developed in many directions, has proved an extremely fruitful one to present-day theoretical thinking.

In the second chapter I mentioned the various ramifications of Erikson's thinking with respect to this concept. At this point I want to return to one of its aspects that seems of fundamental importance.

Erikson (1959) in discussing the development of identity emphasizes that it is only in part a result of actual identification processes. In part it has its roots in *inner sameness and continuity*, which represent another aspect than that of assuredness and identification. This sameness is manifested in congenital behavior attributes. It is manifested in those not yet definable subtle singular characteristics of a person's movements, manners, style.

To this inner sameness comes then what is inculcated by habits, mannerisms, and patterns of behavior from the beginning, even before actual education and acculturation set in, and before any conscious identification takes place.

The identity formation "emerges as an evolving configuration—a configuration which is gradually established by successive ego syntheses and resyntheses throughout childhood; it is a configuration gradually integrating constitutional givens, idiosyncratic libidinal needs, favored capacities, significant identifications, effective defenses, successful sublimations and consistent roles" (p. 116).

The aspect of *inner assuredness* in identity has, according

154

to Erikson, its roots in a "preconscious sense of psycho-social well-being" (p.118).

In the development of this social embeddedness the infant's *trust*, another of Erikson's basic concepts which was introduced before plays the decisive role. In fact, in his book *Young Man Luther* (1958) he speaks of "basic trust" as "the beginning of all sense of identity." "Basic trust" in mutuality is that original "optimism," that assumption that "somebody is there," without which we cannot live" (p. 118).

In a brilliant analysis, Erikson ties basic trust up with *religious faith* and with the ability of religious faith to restore for the young man what the mother did for the infant.

"Trust" or "faith" is moved into the central position for the formation of identity.

What does this mean? Since trust, as Erikson so rightly says, has a foundation in the preconscious, in a basic "optimism," it must of course be conceived of as a primary tendency. It is then, as I pointed out previously (1954), *a primary expectation of a positive reality* into which one may move with trust and not just a reaction to a loving mother. It might be enhanced or weakened by the mother's attitude and behavior, but it is there before, it belongs to the genetic setup anteceding actual contact with the world.

Since, as Erikson also says, this basic trust is "the beginning of all sense of identity," it must belong to the constituents of the same dispositional setup in which "inner sameness and continuity" are given.

Now where exactly does all this lead us? In my opinion, it leads us to a *second basic factor besides "love."*

"Trust" is not "love." It is not a give-and-take in the sense of love, but it is a projection of the self to be responded to from "the other" and from the world outside.

155

An interesting aside to this is Fenichel's (1945) notation at one point when discussing "projection": "A person sensing himself in a landscape *does not simply feel love or hatred for the natural objects, but generally experiences a kind of identification* [italics mine] with the landscape the unio mystica with the father's penis or mother's womb. In general, it may be assumed that in 'consciousness of nature' a projection of the kind described is at work" (p. 206). Projection into nature according to Fenichel may either "connote nature's becoming a representative of our own feelings" or else "nature may also represent another person, and feelings connected with it may have originated in feelings toward a person" (p. 205).

Trust is not love, and trust is basic and primary. To utilize the full scope of this thought, we have to see "trust" in the larger context in which it belongs. Trust is the primary manifestation of what on the conscious level develops into the categories of beliefs. To me this concept represents the missing link in our understanding of the dynamics of motivation. This will I hope become clear when we now study the category that I will call "beliefs," which, as will be shown, plays a fundamental role in human life, comparable only to that of "love."

3.
The Fundamental Role of
Beliefs in Human Life

What exactly are beliefs? Obviously there are many kinds of belief. What are their various functions? Do they have a common denominator? How does it happen that some of

156

them are shrugged off and taken lightly, while others assume an exalted position in people's minds?

It is common to all beliefs that they are developed with regard to things about which we have only incomplete knowledge. Around the questionable data involved in the construct we develop certain mental images.

George Kelly (1955) conceives of these beliefs as *constructs*. He defines them as theories that serve man's need to anticipate the future. He distinguishes *personal* and *scientific* constructs. He says: "Man deals with events by placing constructions upon them," that is, *interpretations* concerning themselves with the future. They result from "an interplay between invention and discovery." Another statement is that "to construe is to see events not merely for what they are, but for the evidence they provide."

Kelly describes the function of psychotherapy as enabling a person to form new constructs after the old ones have proved to be invalid.

Important as this concept of "construct" is, it seems to pertain primarily to the intellectual aspects of beliefs, that is, to the interpretational aspects. Beliefs regarding *values*, which are not separated in Kelly's theory from beliefs regarding *events*, have strongly emotional aspects. It is not the interpretation and anticipation of the future that matter here so much as the conviction giving foundation and certainty to the present.

In Blake and Ramsey's volume, *Perception* (1951), James G. Miller and Else Frenkel-Brunswik go into more detailed discussions of various aspects of belief.

Miller agrees with David Hume in calling belief "an irrational, nonlogical process"; beliefs are conclusions to which one comes by a process of "induction," rather than by "deduction." This process of inductive belief is "jumping to conclusions from inadequate premises" (p. 278).

He sees the main reasons for it in man's need for *protection against ignorance* and from its potential threat, in his *anxiety* with respect to his uncertainty about the external world as well as his anxiety in the presence of ambiguity; in short, in man's insecurity. The concept of tolerance or intolerance of ambiguity was developed by Frenkel-Brunswik (1948, 1949) in her studies on prejudice. The prejudiced person is intolerant of ambiguity and in need of quick conclusions because he is insecure.

I think to these reasons should be added man's genuine interest in *understanding* what is going on in the world, which leads him to experiment with interpretations. These may be recognized to be hypotheses in the more sophisticated thinker while they may take the shape of beliefs with the more naive thinker.

Jean Piaget in several of his brilliant studies gives an abundance of illustrations of children's theorizing and judging based on what they believe is true or right. In his book, *The Construction of Reality in the Child* (1954), he shows belief at work from very early stages on, showing in the behavior of infants who form "constructs" about events.

In our *Inventory of Behavior during the First Year of Life* Hildegard Hetzer and I (1927) found, and later standardized for our baby tests, *searching movements* first occurring with respect to sounds beginning at about two months, searching movements with respect to a disappearing human face at three months, and with respect to a lost toy at five months. Thus, some type of practical "hypothesis" is very early at work in the human child, although it definitely comes later than that "trust" with which the infant, almost im-

158

mediately after it is born, opens its mouth and itself to the world. This trust revealed in the infant's searching movements, as well as in other behavior, like the cuddling up to the mother or moving with hand and feet experimentally out into the world—this trust is a practical manifestation of a positive belief. These movements imply the expectation of good things to be had, of finding acceptance, being wanted in the world. The movements are opposite to those of certain sick children or animals who crawl into a corner and curl up in themselves, offering as little of their surface and openings to the outside world as possible.

The basic trust that somebody is there and cares comes, in my opinion, long before such feelings as "being thrown into existence." This existentialistic formulation of our human helplessness seems to me a sophisticated, not a primary experience.

The belief expressed in theoretical constructs is of a different kind than that which underlies "trust." It expresses a *hopeful confidence* that one is right in claiming one knows how things really are and that the future will bring *confirmative support*. This support might be hoped for in terms of wishful thinking. But the hopeful confidence might also be a well-based belief in the future of the self. Then again, it might express itself in self-limiting humble bowing to "God's will" or to fate or even to a master of one's fate.[3] Thomas

3. This "hopeful confidence" and even more, an attitude we will call "identifying conviction" is what in religious language is usually spoken of as "faith." I agree with Ekstein (1958) in his discussion of Paul Bergman's (1958) paper that "faith" is not really identical with "trust." On the other hand, I feel that trust is primary and more basic than faith, which, while it may be blind and primitive, still implies an element of conviction. This already presupposes some ego structure. Trust to me is an originally unconscious anticipation of things to come, which may then become conscious. Faith to me is a specific belief.

But of course, at the present stage of investigation this is still partly a

M. French demonstrated in brilliant studies (1952) the integrative role of "hope."

The opposite is that skepticism and doubt, which under unfavorable circumstances develops early in children who feel they cannot trust anything their environment promises or says or may do.

> "My mother," says Roger, now thirty-nine, "had terrible moods. As a little boy of three and four, I was already aware of them, and whenever she called me or I saw her coming, I was at once on my guard and tried to find out in what mood she might be."

This distrust, applied to information obtained from adults, was drastically expressed in a group of difficult boys about whom Dr. Lawrence Mathae, one of the members of our previously mentioned Value Study Group, reported.

> "What is for real?" was the frequent question of these teen-agers, members of a therapy group. "I mean what is for really real?" some would add.

Dr. Mathae felt they endowed reality with an extremely high value and they want to be sure they know the truth about it; because, I would add, they feel that they often have been deceived.

Both the hopeful confidence of constructs and identifying convictions pertain to theoretical aspect of beliefs, while trust is activating, dynamic, and actually motivating.

> A good example of the difference between trust and belief is the previously presented case of Barbara. Barbara started out with full trust in her parents. She opened herself

---

problem of language and of definition. Like Ekstein I feel it would serve the clarity of our thinking, if we reserved the word faith for beliefs that, like religious faith, imply convictions, while there is no such commitment stipulated in the concept of trust.

160

to what they taught her about a good child's obedience to her parents and her church and she acted upon these teachings.

When later it appeared that her devotion did not find full acknowledgment nor lead to success, the motivating power of her trust was exhausted.

She still did not give up her beliefs, that is her hopeful confidence that confirmative support could only come within this system she had been taught. But her beliefs had dwindled down to a theoretical construct. She could no more act on their strength because something had been faulty with the way she had activated her trust: she did not know what.

The reason Barbara clung to her beliefs was that she did not find any other constructs acceptable and she could not, like other disillusioned youths, for example the beatniks, live in an "existential vacuum," as Frankl calls the state of having no belief at all.

The case of Barbara shows a further aspect of beliefs. Barbara not only entrusted herself and had a hopeful confidence, but went one step further, she had an *identifying conviction* regarding the *validity* of the religious and moral philosophy in which she had been brought up. Her conviction embraced belief in her parents' teachings regarding child-parent relationships as well as belief in her church's teachings regarding moral conduct and metaphysical doctrine.

When she had lost her motivating and activating trust in her relationship with her family, she still held on to her metaphysical beliefs, because she needed an existential frame of reference.

The decisive reason for Barbara's identification, particularly with her mother, was undoubtedly *love*. But she also had *belief*. To start with, Barbara had both love for and

161

belief in her parents. We have other examples in which identification is based solely on one or the other:

> Myrna, now a woman in her forties, remembers in psychotherapy that at the age of four years she made a definite difference between her love for her mother and her admiration for and *belief* in a female neighbor. (The details of this situation were given in Chapter 3.) The child found that the neighbor represented a model in terms of values that Myrna believed in and identified with. The neighbor was admirable and an ideal that Myrna could follow, due to her own gifts and inclinations.
> Yet she went on loving her mother for whom she became increasingly sorry. She felt there was something pitiful about her mother whom she surrounded gradually with a kind of protective care.

My assumption that identifying convictions may develop out of a previously vindicated belief (trust, hopeful confidence) just as well as out of love has been proved correct in a number of cases.

First, we saw in the case of Barbara that she loses most of her identifying conviction and in fact much of her identity after her trust and hopeful confidence have failed her. Yet she goes on loving.

Another case may be quoted in which no identity development at all could take place:

> Amy, now a divorced woman in her thirties, had an early childhood determined by only one goal: *to be good and avoid angering her mother* who punished her without mercy for the smallest misdemeanors. Amy loved her mother, but a stronger feeling was her fear. Fear and avoidance of punishment were all that Amy could think of for years, and as a result she actually had no identity, no goals. The first man who wanted to marry her, she accepted and entered into a meaningless marriage mostly to get away from home.

162

If wanting to get away from home and have a different life may be called a goal, it is that of a negative identity born out of fear and without any concrete envisagement of the future.

Identifying conviction is the foundation on which religious faith and the acceptance of religious or other dogmas rest. It has a stronger motivating and activating power than a mere theory, because usually it encompasses trust.

Besides providing an identity for the individual, convictions, insofar as they are beliefs, are correlated with specific values. For example, a person who has a strong conviction against capital punishment might be said to place a high value on human life.

The ability of belief with which we are born and which allows us to develop trust, confidence, and convictions, leads us finally to what was introduced in Chapter 3 under the discussion of *self-assessment* and assessment of others. We are motivated to this assessment by "conscience" and by our self's tendency to an integrated inner order. Conscience as used here, is not identical with the superego, which makes us bow to society's demands. "Conscience" is a word we use as the name for man's own inner calling to be his best self.

In religious dogmas or philosophical theories human beings try to find coherent expression and justifying reasoning for their beliefs, which they feel compelled to bring into meaningful systems. The foregoing considerations are the reason why we think that *belief* and *love* (including social relatedness) represent two fundamentally different approaches to life. The motivating goal of our beliefs is to establish our existence, to try for *certitude*; the motivating goal of our love is to find *union* with the rest of the world through a give-and-take relationship.

On the different developmental levels formed by the successively predominating four basic tendencies, belief and love operate in the direction of successively different subgoals. A tentative schematic representation of the development of "belief" and "love" as related to the four basic tendencies is given in Table 4.

4.
The Concept of Value Potential

The individual's identity as it exists at any point of his development represents what I propose to call this person's *value potential*. This concept may be paralleled to the concept of an individual's *insight potential*.

The ability of an individual to develop adequate insight is gauged by many psychotherapists as part of their diagnostic appraisal of the chances of therapeutic success.

The estimate of the value potential would permit corresponding considerations with respect to a person's ability to develop an adequate set of values.

I define the value potential as the range of values an individual is able to encompass, in terms of *awareness, appreciation, acceptance, and activation.* By "ability" I mean a functional aptitude, determined by innate potentials as well as by experience and learning (emotional and motivational development).

A person's value potential may be comprehensive or limited, depending on the individual's own basic tendencies, on what has been brought to his attention during his lifetime, and on the degree of freedom of action that his emotional balance permits.

164

Table 4—"Belief" and "Love" as Related to the Four Basic Tendencies

Basic Tendencies	Behavior	Motivating subgoal	Behavior	Motivating subgoal	Endgoal
	Belief	Certitude	Love	Union	Fulfillment
Need-satisfaction	Trust	Anchorage	Attachment	Comfort, happiness	Well-being
Self-limiting adaptation	Hopeful confidence	Confirmative support	Dependence, independence	Security and integrity	Survival
Creative expansion	Identifying conviction	Identity, values	Generating (reproduction, production)	Products, accomplishment	Self-realization
Upholding of the internal order	Self-assessment, assessment	Conscience, integratedness	Charity	Participating in humanity	Worth
Fulfillment	Religion, philosophy	Meaningful system	Mystical oneness	Merging into universe	Serenity

The value potential is then a *function* of the innate and experientially developed structure of a person's basic tendencies. An individual whose basic tendencies show a good equilibrium and are well integrated has the greatest possible value potential, because this person can appreciate, accept, and activate the values of pleasure and comfort, of fitting in and belonging, of creating and accomplishing, of functioning in an orderly way, and of having peace of mind. An individual whose basic tendencies are in unequilibrium and not integrated has a limited value potential, because of an exclusive or predominant tendency in one or the other direction.

Of course we have to appreciate the fact that in most individuals there exists a *hierarchical* order as far as their values are concerned, whether they know it or not. But in the well-adjusted person whose basic tendencies are in equilibrium, there is no rigidity regarding this hierarchy. They want an all-round fulfillment, and they can temporarily switch from emphasizing one particular value to any of the others more readily than other persons. That is to say they may at one time want more than anything to accomplish something worthwhile, then they want more than anything to have a period of pleasure, of vacation, of relaxation, then may come a period in which they are concerned with their duties to their family and their friends then they may want to meditate and concentrate on problems of their own inner peace of mind.

The predominance and exclusiveness of one over all other values or the complete disregard of one as against all other values is the result of an unequilibrium among the basic tendencies.

Linda, whose story was presented in previous chapters, is a case in point of a comprehensive value potential due to nearly equally strong adaptive as well as creative tendencies, which she was able to pursue in alternation depending on her circumstances. Since Linda liked her family and liked to help them she did not mind the idea of temporarily postponing her own more creative development. Another person with a more imperative creative urge might have resented the years of loss of its development.

Another case may demonstrate an extremely limited value potential that was more and more narrowed down in the course of a very neurotic development.

Ben was a man of fifty when he entered psychotherapy. He suffered from depression and a number of psychosomatic symptoms, such as constant fatigue and frequent headaches. He also suffered from impotence. He was a twice-divorced, childless salesman who lived a rather unsocial lonely life.

He explained his depression as due to his meaningless, empty life, about which he felt guilty. He felt that he had wasted his life in pursuit of worthless goals in which he did not believe. He had started on a career that meant nothing, had run businesses and had taken jobs that he did not like, had married haphazardly without love. The one thing that meant anything to him, his desire to write, he had neglected to develop. The reason he gave for this neglect was that he did not really believe in his ability, although admittedly he had twice had two short stories published. He thought that psychotherapy might help him, even though it was somewhat late in his life to pull himself out of his dragging existence and to enable him to develop his writing talent or to do something better with himself. He was intelligent enough to recognize that his impotence had to do with the self-contempt with which he lived.

Ben worked through the dynamics of his early childhood very successfully and even enthusiastically for about a year. The beginning of his unhappiness dated back to his fifth year when his mother who had spoiled and doted on him, her first son, had died in childbirth of her fourth child, and Ben found himself exposed to a harsh and unloving world.

His father had always favored his little girls, while he was a disciplinarian to his only son. The "mama's boy" did not take well to the demands made on him by the strict father nor later to those made by his teachers. He developed a strong opposition to both parent and teachers and spent his time in daydreaming.

In exploring his past during his psychotherapy, Ben recognized that his whole development throughout life had been determined by his opposition to his father and his wishful thinking of himself back in a time where he was given his mother's doting love.

Although highly intelligent, Ben made only average or below-average grades in school because he resented his father pushing him, and his sarcastic remarks. He did not finish high school and refused to go to college, getting himself a succession of clerical jobs so as to make himself as independent from his father as he possibly could. He also admitted in therapy that he wanted to hurt his father's pride and crush his hopes for his brilliant son's future. Only after his father's death did Ben, who was then in his twenties, go back to school. In the shortest possible time, he finished high school and went to college where he took a degree in law. For some time he practiced law until he was offered a partnership in a firm, which he and his partner ran for a couple of years none too successfully. After they sold out, Ben took managerial jobs in other firms, but he never had his heart in any of these things.

At heart he was a scholar and writer, and he grieved forever that he did not get beyond haphazard attempts to pursue his real interests.

In one area Ben was enabled to make true progress during his psychotherapy: he became able to love for the first time in his life and developed a very happy affair in which his potency was stronger than ever.

But his attempts to write failed tragically. He was unable to generate the continued mental effort that this work required. His comfort meant too much to him and he had acquired too deeply rooted habits of play and relaxation to extricate himself for any length of time. His hopeless struggle against himself brought him a new type of unhappiness after self-understanding and love had freed him from his previous depression. Unable to resign himself to the acceptance of the fact that his development had led to a reduction of his original potentiality, he spent much of his free time in fruitless attempts at writing while at other times he struggled to overcome his regrets and to find peace of mind.

Perhaps the car accident in which he died was not quite as accidental as it seemed. It was a merciful ending to a rather hopeless life.

This case demonstrates a limited value potential due to a neurotic development. This man, after a lifetime of stubborn self-indulgence and poor adaptation, was no longer capable of developing his creative potential. From a detailed study of his case history, it became quite evident that his basic tendencies were initially less unbalanced and his value potential was originally much more comprehensive. Some twenty years earlier psychotherapy could very probably have helped him to an adequately fulfilling life.

In other types of cases, the value potential seems limited from the start. An outstanding example is found in the *hypersensitive* individual. Hypersensitivity is one of the few generally acknowledged hereditary dispositions. Its primary origin and the difficulties encountered in preventing its development or in treating it later, have been discussed by Gabriel Langfeldt (1951).

From the beginning, the hypersensitive infant is constantly overexcited, shocked, and disturbed by stimuli that the average child can take in his stride. His continuous frustration requires a continuous struggle for adjustment. Then, he is so preoccupied with efforts to satisfy his unsatisfied needs and to adapt himself to the onslaught experienced from his environment that he hardly ever gets to develop his creative potential adequately or to maintain his internal order for any length of time.

These are the people who long for peace of mind more than anything in the world or who forever cry over not having been loved enough by their mothers.

These individuals serve as examples that there are innate, as well as experientially conditioned, limitations to what a person can do or to his ability to bring values to materialization. We do not share the optimism, which seems rather widely spread, that by means of psychotherapy or due to a decision to give life a meaning or to find the right meaning for one's life (V. E. Frankl), everybody can be enabled to actually live meaningfully.

There are many mental and physical impairments such as inadequacy, defective equipment, or acquired defectiveness, advanced and protracted neurotic conditions, or extremely unfavorable conditions of life that might prohibit meaningful living and might limit the fulfillment of values to the attainment of only the smallest accomplishments.

Some psychoanalytic thinkers feel that the concepts of ego ideals and ego strength should suffice to determine a person's ability of awareness, appreciation, acceptance, and activation of values. However, Heinz Hartmann (1959) points out how problematic the concept of ego strength actually is:

> I stress again that no satisfactory definition of the concepts of ego strength and ego weakness is feasible without taking into account the nature and maturational stage of

the ego apparatuses which underlie intelligence, will, and action (p. 107).

It is just this "nature and maturational stage" that I undertook to categorize with the four basic tendencies I postulated. Their equilibrium and integration determines the value-potential, not only on the conscious ego level but even earlier on the level of preconscious tendencies. In view of its clarity and comprehensiveness, value-potential seems a useful concept.

The idea of "potentials" in terms of limitations is objectionable to some therapists. But actually they refer to such limitations more often than they are aware of.

Thus, a famous psychoanalyst whom I asked if she got a certain patient of hers far enough to get married, answered: "What else did you expect me to do?" This was actually a referral to a limited goal- or value-potential.

6   *Values in Psychotherapy*

1.
Values and the Goal of Psychotherapy

In more recent discussions of the goal of psychotherapy two different aspects are emphasized by several authors.

One group stresses that after psychotherapy the patient should be "getting along" more satisfactorily (Lorand, 1946) or that he should be coping more effectively with life "with a minimum of excess baggage, that is, repressions, feelings of inferiority, of anxiety, and so on" (Clara Thompson, 1950, p. 242).

Another group stresses that the patient should be "free for a creative expansion of his personality and for striving for self-realization" (Fromm-Reichmann, 1956, p. 16). They speak of evoking the "constructive use" of "assets and possibilities" (John C. Whitehorn, 1956) or of releasing a "constructive tendency" (Rogers, 1956).

172

Clara Thompson summarizes her comparison of Sullivan and Fromm in that she finds, "Sullivan concerns himself more with helping the patient to see how his defense machinery (security operation) works to the detriment of effective loving, while Fromm attempts to cut through the defenses to communicate with the underlying constructive forces, leaving the security operations to fall by the wayside" (p. 169).

Wolberg (1954) seems to feel that the coping, the optimal functioning within given limitations, represents a "practical" goal to which the therapist might have to limit himself at times, as he cannot always hope to accomplish "ideal" objectives of mental health, to enable the patient "to plan creatively and realistically, and to execute his plans in accordance with existent opportunities" (pp. 553-554).

This means that some therapists consider it a sufficient goal and success if their patients can handle their given difficulties as they arise, while other therapists want to free in their patients a creative orientation toward the future. The one does not necessarily follow from the other, as becomes very clear in Wolberg's separation of the "practical" and the "ideal" goal. That is to say, a person is not necessarily enabled to develop toward self-realization by being enabled to cope with given difficulties.

This raises two questions: What exactly is amiss in the purely adjusted functioning, what more does a person need to develop creatively? Can the purely adjustment type of functioning ever be considered as a satisfactory cure?

A very thoughtful more recent Round Table Discussion (1956) of the goals of therapy by a group of psychiatrists who represent a holistic point of view, many of them followers of Karen Horney, impresses one with its human understanding and the wide range as well as flexibility of considerations.

The common denominator for this group whose moderator was H. Kelman (1956) is the striving to help the patient to self-realization. "Relief of mental or psychosomatic symptoms" and "adjustment" are rejected as goals by Frederick Weiss. Nathan Ackermann, in discussing the criteria of a successful "cure" states that ultimately there is no healthy emotional living without values, and he agrees with Burgum that values are realized only if there is "appropriate action toward common good."

Harold Kelman and Oskar Diethelm emphasize how goals of therapy have been shifting recently toward the direction of enabling the patient to master his life and himself more satisfactorily. Oskar Diethelm illustrates some of the more recent ideas:

> Instead of freedom from anxiety, which is still the goal for many psychiatrists, the ability to bear this painful experience is stressed by others. A similar change has become obvious in the evaluation of frustration and aggressive impulses. Increasingly one tries to make the patient aware of his limitations and on such a basis to bear frustration, to accept one's hostility and be able to deal constructively with one's aggressive impulses, and to recognize and tolerate one's weaknesses. The importance of insight has been considered by many authors, and it is now accepted that the goal of therapy should not be to give insight into the dynamics but to provide understanding and ability to deal with oneself and with reality situations (p. 5).

To me it seems doubtful that any human being can ever be satisfied with just "functioning" and "coping" with difficulties as they arise. A person cannot live for long without goals and without hope and be happy or even content. He needs a future to look forward to, to believe in, to build on. In my opinion merely coping with current problems is no goal, and adjustment is not enough.

174

What is then the "more" that a person needs to be enabled not only to function adequately under given circumstances, but to become future-directed and oriented toward self-realization, creative expansion, or whatever we want to call it?

He needs to have goals, directedness toward these goals, the ability of integrated functioning, the freedom to make decisions and to act accordingly.

Values are potential goals. But there are also many values without any relationship to potential goals, values that block a person's goal development or that become completely out of reach because of a person's faulty goal development.

There are many things that one might find of value to do or to have without necessarily aspiring to them oneself. One might think it valuable to create art, to have a collection of works of art, to be able to do a lot of traveling, or to acquire and have great wealth without necessarily wishing any of these things for oneself.

One can, on the other hand, have values that block one's own goal development. Some people value unobtainable possessions or abilities to the detriment of what they have, so that what they have appears of little value to them.

Furthermore, a person may get entangled in the pursuit of goals that are far removed from the values he believes in. An example of this was given in the case of Ben.

The case of Barbara, which was presented more fully, showed the emergence of an unrealistic value and goal pattern out of a specific background. The perfectionism with which she adhered to her rigorous concept of the demands of her Church and with which she set up the standard that a man had to live up to for her to find him acceptable represented a rather unrealistic outlook on the future. While she gradually was able to get over the hurt of her past and acquire enough insight to acknowledge the excessiveness and even the rigidity of her demands on herself and on life, she was slow in setting up goals in a new direction.

It was the therapist's decision not to intervene in her slow progress, rather to consider the acquired insight, the gradual overcoming of the past emotional injury, the beginning of compromises, and the first attempts at new goal-setting as the optimum that could be achieved for the present. The reason this seemed the most constructive position to take under the circumstances was that this girl's integrity seemed completely tied up with the standard and code of ethics of her Church. This seemed more what she wanted to live for than anything else.

Here we again return to the problem of the therapist's judgment.

2.
Values in Different Psychotherapeutic Systems

Although a value problem may require a psychotherapist's personal judgment, he can of course first rely to a lesser or greater extent on the directives that he receives from the psychotherapeutic system to which he adheres.

Considerable attention is recently being paid to the different value implications inherent in the different psychotherapeutic theories. Several authors of articles in the recent book *Psychoanalysis and Human Values*, edited by J. H. Masserman (1960) contributed findings and observations in these directions.

Fritz C. Redlich, for example, discusses the fact that different cultures seem to take to different psychotherapeutic systems depending on how the "institutional values of the system correspond to the institutional values of the culture" (p. 90). He sees the explanation:

> . . . why Morita in Japan developed a psychotherapy which is closely related to certain Zen practices, why Nationalist Socialist psychiatry espoused genetics, or why Iron Curtain countries reject our psychodynamic and psychosocial theories. It also attempts to explain why dogmatic and doctrinal religious and political systems are incompatible with psychoanalytic propositions. The critical and negative implications of the basic psychoanalytic propositions are too threatening for any rigid and dogmatic system. If the institutional values of a given system, e.g., psychoanalysis, do not enhance the political or religious system, e.g., communism or fundamentalist religions, they are rejected and branded as false and dangerous. We encounter a similar difficulty with patients who adhere rigidly to a dogmatic system; they are rarely suited for analysis (pp. 90-91).

Freud himself did not think of psychoanalysis in terms of a *Weltanschauung*.

> Psychoanalysis is not in my opinion in a condition to create a *Weltanschauung* of its own. It has no need to do so, for it is a branch of science and can subscribe to the scientific *Weltanschauung*. The latter, however, hardly merits such a high sounding name, for it does not take everything into its scope. It is incomplete and makes no claim to be comprehensive or to constitute a system (Freud, 1932).

Redlich feels that there is a definite reason that psychoanalysis is so popular with certain social and educational groups in the United States in contrast to other countries, where this theory and therapy meet with much greater resistance.

> My explanation pointed to the fact that psychoanalysis as a science and method of treatment seems to satisfy the

177

needs of a certain segment of the North American population for a rational and just orientation to life and also fulfills their demands in a rapidly changing, restless society which has lost confidence in some of its important values and beliefs and is groping for a new identity (p. 90).

Some of the changes that took place in psychoanalysis when transferred from the Viennese to the American culture, will be discussed in a special section by Rudolf Ekstein (pp. oooff.).

The great importance attributed to the *individual person* in terms of the length of time devoted to the minute study of his problem is a feature of psychoanalysis against which I heard objections raised in certain parts of Europe. Redlich also makes the point that a "relatively individualistic and comfort-loving culture such as that of the United States is apt to take to this type of treatment" (p. 97).

As Redlich points out, the psychoanalytic emphasis on *truth* is something that not everybody is up to.

This is undoubtedly true. Yet it seems to me that Freud's emphasis on the self-deception under which we suffer due to unconscious repression has become so much a matter of general knowledge and awareness, that one can actually speak of the pre-Freudian and the post-Freudian personality with respect to the acknowledgement of this human trait in oneself as well as in others.

This acknowledgment, as well as the willingness and ability to inquire into it, to *think things through*, which is the main prerequisite and tool of all analytically oriented therapy, presupposes as Redlich also points out a somewhat scientifically oriented mind. The analytic is a rational approach to the self differing from those techniques that like Zen Buddhism, Carl Jung's analytic theory, and some of the followers of existentialism include mystical and philosophical speculations.

This reliance on intellectual methods of self-understanding is in part responsible for those social limitations of the use of the analytic therapy which Redlich and Hollingshead (1958) established.

As for the rest, it does not seem easy to point out exactly what values Redlich's system emphasizes. He mentions the following contradictory interpretations:

One of the most quoted formulations documenting Freud's belief in reason is the famous quotation. "Where the id was ego shall be." This statement is taken by Fromm and also by many others as an expression of Freud's anti-instinctual viewpoint. It is interesting that Freud was also blamed for the opposite tendency, an immoral hedonism, and for the promotion of "will" over intellect in the sense of Schopenhauer and Nietzsche (p. 92).

Redlich himself does not see the ego as an anti-instinctual force, but considers its central functions to be the "reconciliation of the demands of reality with the pressure of instincts and also the superego" (p. 93). He agrees with Marcuse that "Freud conceived of an incessant struggle between instincts, between the forces of life and death, and between the inner strivings and the environment, which man encounters and creates," and that there is *no room for ideology*. As Marcuse (1955) points out this is differently seen by the "revisionists," particularly by Erich Fromm (1958) who professes a *definite ideology* and wants to establish a better world.

Redlich sees differing values in the group of those psychiatrists whose orientation is "analytic and psychological" as against those whose orientation is "directive and organic." I wonder whether this division necessarily represents different values, except with respect to the *authoritarian* approach. But then there exist also authoritarian psychoanalysts whose interpretations become dictates. To me the difference between the "D-O" and the "A-P" group, as Redlich calls them, is not so much one of values as one of conceptions of illness.

However, the fact that different socioeconomic groups of patients conceive of their illness as emotional or as due to objective factors, seems more significant when one regards the importance they attribute to both.

This difference among our patients is seen from another angle by Donald A. Bloch. In an article appearing in the same volume as Redlich's (1960), Bloch cites from Redlich and Hollingshead's study the distinction of "maturity values" and of "success values" that determine the attitude to mental-health work. The mental-health worker is apt to be influenced by this difference of emphasis.

Bloch finds in reviewing the literature that therapists in general evaluate the mental health of their patients with respect to a specific type and number of variables. He mentions as the most important: *satisfaction* experienced in activities and relationships, degree of *involvement* in activities and relationships, *range of interests*, *degree of control* over behavior and use of skills and resources, *tenor of behavior* or emotional tone, *autonomy of behavior*, and *insight*.

In these terms would be described the picture of the *desirable personality*, which therapists generally seem to aim at. Bloch sees in this list the variables delineating "the desirable qualities of the rising young executive, of the organization man, or the upwardly mobile middle class citizen" (p. 120).

It is true that this is the picture of a well-nourished, pragmatically oriented, and probably successful human who is neither bothered by the labor pains of creative work, nor by philosophical incertitude regarding the worthwhileness of his doings and existence.

Georgene Seward (in press), who interviewed sixty-five psychotherapists of varying, mostly analytic schools, finds that the classical Freudians do not on the whole concern themselves with value problems, that "insight" and "social adjustment" is still their most frequently quoted goal of therapy. Other therapeutic groups concern themselves with values and strive to accomplish self-acceptance as well as self-realization.

The following section by Dr. Rudolf Ekstein, who was an active participant in the psychoanalytic movement in Vienna and is now practicing in the United States, concerns itself with the values in a specific psychotherapeutic system as related to changes in the social matrix out of which it developed.

3.
Rudolf Ekstein, Ph.D.,[4] *on*
Reflections on Parallels in the Therapeutic and
the Social Process[5]

The goal of dynamically oriented psychotherapies such as psychoanalysis has frequently been described as the restoration of inner freedom, of capacity for choice. The emotionally or mentally ill person is seen as oppressed by symptoms, dominated by inhibitions, anxieties or archaic and impulsive behavior patterns which have destroyed the purposes of age-appropriate choice. This manner of speaking borrows its

---

4. Coordinator of Training and Research, Reiss-Davis Clinic for Child Guidance, Los Angeles, California.

5. From a lecture to the Psychiatry Forum of the Menninger School of Psychiatry on April 13, 1960, Topeka, Kansas.

metaphors and similes from the social sciences, from political philosophy and is related to the values of Western civilization. Social theories of change, like therapeutic theories of change, have moved through a variety of stages and it may well be worth while to compare certain changes in theory and technique in these two areas of human endeavor in order to reflect on certain parallels in the therapeutic and in the social process. For purposes of simplification only psychoanalytic theory and technique will be considered.

In 1886 when Freud returned from the Salepetrière and his experience with the great Charcot, he brought his teacher's notions back to Vienna. He thought then of hypnosis as a means which would help people in psychic distress, in states of emotional emergency. He hoped to help the patient who came to him with deep-seated conflicts which were frequently experienced and expressed as anxiety states, as panics, or through hysterical symptoms, by means of hypnosis, that is, by creating a psychological situation where he was to take over completely. He represented, as it were, the auxilliary self of the patient. This auxilliary self included what would be described today as the auxilliary ego as well as the authoritative super-ego, authority playing such an important role in the hypnotic process. At that time the psychotherapeutic process, precursor as it was of genuine psychoanalysis, was seen as a hypnotic situation in which the patient was helped to face what he could not face alone and without help, that is, the unconscious conflict, that which was pushed out, kept in a state of repression in order to avoid the pain of unresolvable conflict. It seems then that the therapist at that time acted like a benevolent parent-surrogate, who helped the patient to relive the conflict and to thus free himself from its pathological force. One is reminded of a famous simile which Freud used. He suggested that at the end of a treatment phase the unconscious conflict emerges but has not any longer a pathological effect on the patient, just as the mummy that the archaeologist excavates falls to dust as it is exposed to the light of day. These early notions assumed an unconscious which was viewed as a "seething cauldron," as a revolutionary, impulsive and uncontrolled mass which threatened or overpowered the reasonable equilibrium of the personality. The cure was pictured as the kind of help in which these seething masses emerge from the slums of the unconscious, come to the well-controlled foreground of consciousness and give up the useless, neurotic struggle.

Hypnotic treatment soon was given up by Freud, since he realized that the method of hypnotic catharsis did not bring forth sure and lasting results. Could he have thought of many a short-lived revolt in Europe such as, for example, the aborted German revolution of 1848? With his patients, in any case, after the initial catharsis, the symptoms returned, and Freud realized that cure would prove impossible unless the waking person could fully participate in the cure. He demonstrated that cure which was based on only catharsis and hypnosis cannot be more than temporary. He then introduced free association, a completely new method in which there was collaboration of a different nature between him and the patient. He gave up being the power which works through suggestion and hypnosis. He made the patient into a collaborator, someone who free-associated by conscious choice and who actively participated in the process. This method yielded better results. These results in turn invited constant technical changes, since as we know Freud soon discovered that the new method of psychoanalysis could work only if he not only interpreted the deeper meaning of the material which the

183

patient brought to him but interpreted as well those aspects of the patient's productions which opposed the emergence of unconscious material. The analysis of the resistance, of the defensive and of the adaptive struggle developed. As these new methods were introduced, the theory changed as well. At first we utilized the theory in which we spoke about the unconscious, the preconscious and the conscious forces; then we added the notions of dream and censorship. Around 1923 the tripartite model of ego, super-ego, and id was introduced, which led to a way of analyzing data in which different parts of the psychic organization are considered. The goal of the analysis was no longer just to make the unconscious conscious. It was not only catharsis, not only making alive what was buried, but it was also to study, to understand all the processes, all the methods which had been used to maintain the unconscious conflict in a state of repression. The analysis of the transference and resistances, the analysis of character structure was slowly being developed. Each change in technique suggested changes in theory and vice versa. Thus the theory changed considerably and we finally came to a point where we discovered that we not only need to know about the unconscious, the forces of repression, but that we also need to consider the functions of the ego which make for character changes and character structure. We then proceeded to consider these forces in the ego which are comparatively free of conflict, and free of the effect of unconscious struggle, forces which make up important aspects of the personality and participate in its functioning and in the resolution of neurotic and psychotic illness. Thus we have now a change in theoretical assumptions and in the selection of available observations which is sometimes expressed in terms of the early stress on instinct theory, the later stress on the

184

psychic apparatus, and currently the stress on ego psychology.

All this, of course, is quite familiar and is only repeated in order to allow us to see these issues in a new context. It has been frequently stated that psychoanalytic scientific language has benefited from metaphoric language which is derived from other sciences. Usually we refer to physiology, to biology, to physics and other notions from nineteenth century science in order to make this point. Contributions such as Colby's *Energy and Structure in Psychoanalysis* (1955) suggest to us that a good many psychoanalytic concepts are in urgent need of revision today, since they are based on analogies which come from sciences, the theoretical concepts of which were developed at the turn of the century but which are outdated and outmoded today. I do not share this point of view, since the usefulness of an analogy does not depend on its original meaning in the science from which it is derived. I want to turn the reader's attention to a type of analogy which Freud and later analysts used and to which we do not always pay as much attention as we well might. I am referring to all these metaphors and allegories, to these analogies which Freud and other psychoanalysts have used and which are derived from the social sciences or from social context. These are the analogies which remind us of the social process. It seems appropriate, if we remind ourselves of certain risks in the use of analogies. Analogies may be both useful and dangerous. The physicist J. Robert Oppenheimer, in an address before the American Psychological Association (1955), spoke about the concern of the psychologists for their language, so often metaphoric or based on analogy. The psychologists frequently look to the physical sciences for a scientific standard, while feeling that psychiatry and psychology have not yet freed their concept from metaphor and analogy. Oppenheimer stated:

What I am going to talk about is analogy as an instrument in science and, to a much lesser extent, some slight traits of analogies between the sciences; mostly the second theme has led to misunderstanding and limitation; as for the first theme, analogy is indeed an indispensible, an inevitable tool for scientific progress. Perhaps I had better say what I mean by that. I do not mean metaphor; I do not mean allegory; I do not even mean similarity; but I mean a special kind of similarity which is the similarity of structure, the similarity of form, a similarity of constellation between two sets of structures, two sets of particulars that are manifestly very different but have structural parallels. It has to do with relation and inter-connection.

Let us then look at some of the analogies between the psychotherapeutic process and psychoanalytic theory on the one hand and the social process and social theories on the other. Some of these analogies might better be termed similarities or parallels in Oppenheimer's terms. As was suggested earlier, psychotherapy, before the turn of the century, the first kind of psychotherapy as practiced, for example, by Freud and Breuer, was hypnosis. Hypnosis invites the analogy of the hypnotist as a benevolent ruler. Some of the emperors at the turn of the century in Europe thought of themselves and were thought of as benevolent emperors, as enlightened absolute rulers whose goal it was to improve the lot of the masses who lived in misery. One is reminded of Freud's comment (1918) that "we shall probably discover that the poor are even less ready to part with their neurosis than the rich, because the hard life that awaits them if they recover offers them no attraction, and illness gives them one more claim to social help. Perhaps, we may only be able to achieve anything by combining mental assistance with some material support, in the manner of Emperor Josef." The broad masses,

186

living in unhappiness and social misery, would look happily to such a paternalistic system, a process of social change through the method of "Father Knows Best." This method never worked for very long with the emperors and did not guarantee constructive and peaceful change. The social system of absolute monarchies in Europe slowly and sometimes violently gave way to other forms of social control. Therapeutic methods based on hypnosis primarily did not work permanently for patients and hypnosis was given up as well. One might go even further in tracing this parallel and suggest that just as there are sometimes revivals of paternalistic systems, we find that in psychotherapy too hypnosis too is occasionally benefiting from a revival of interest in its use. In the social process we speak of a falling back to earlier form of social control, while in the psychotherapeutic process, as earlier techniques are adopted again, we may speak of regression.

At the turn of the century then we are confronted with the greatest work that Freud has given us, *The Interpretation of Dreams* (1900). We find in this work many analogies which are derived from social or political situations. The dream work is described as the attempt of the dreamer to hide from censorship the latent dream thoughts behind the manifest dream content. Freud directly compares dream censorship to social or political censorship. He says:

> A similar difficulty confronts the political writer who has disagreeable truths to tell to those in authority. If he presents them undisguised, the authorities will suppress his words—after they have been spoken, if his pronouncement was an oral one, but beforehand, if he had intended to make it in print. A writer must beware of the censorship, and on its account he must soften and distort the expression

of his opinion. According to the strength and sensitiveness of the censorship he finds himself compelled either merely to refrain from certain forms of attack, or to speak in allusions in place of direct references, or he must conceal his objectionable pronouncement beneath some apparently innocent disguise: for instance, he may describe a dispute between two Mandarins in the Middle Kingdom, when the people he really has in mind are officials in his own country. The stricter the censorship, the more far-reaching will be the disguise and the more ingenious too may be the means employed for putting the reader on the scent of the true meaning.

The fact that the phenomena of censorship and of dream distortion correspond down to their smallest details justifies us in presuming that they are similarly determined.

Clinical literature, while accepting the similarities between dream censorship and political censorship, frequently does not make clear its dissimilarities, such as when the notions of repression and suppression are not differentiated. Freud in 1900 set himself the task to study the techniques employed in order to get around the dream censorship. This censorship is seen as a guard at the door that keeps the repression in force; this guard stands there with threatening devices which are to increase anxiety like the border guard who is to watch the frontier between two countries and who requires legitimate papers of him who wishes to pass from one country into the other. The passport had to be accepted by the censorship; its content had to be admissible. The forbidden thought was to be admitted into "civilized society," even if papers had to be forged in order to get by the censorship, and pass as "innocent."

Another example from Freud is to stress his awareness of the use of analogy. He writes:

If this picture of the true psychical agencies and their relation to consciousness is accepted, there is a complete analogy in political life to the extraordinary affection which I felt in my dream for my friend R., who was treated with such contumely during the dream's interpretation. Let us imagine a society in which a struggle is in process between a ruler who is jealous of his power and an alert public opinion. The people are in revolt against an unpopular official and demand his dismissal. But the autocrat, to show that he need take no heed of the popular wish, chooses that moment for bestowing a high distinction upon the official, though there is no other reason for doing so. In just the same way my second agency, which commands the approaches to consciousness, distinguished my friend R. by a display of excessive affection simply because the wishful impulses belonging to the first system, for particular reasons of their own on which they were intent at the moment, choose to condemn him as a simpleton.

In 1923 Freud introduced the tripartite model of the psychic apparatus. In using this model he no longer speaks about the id as the seething cauldron which constantly tries to push to the foreground. One is tempted to think of the revolution in Central Europe of 1918 as having then passed, and of the new conditions which gave the Central European countries a democratic constitution, a republican form of government. Reorganization had taken place and, instead of the seething cauldron which was slowly destroying the Central European empires, new forms of social solutions were attempted. The tripartite model of ego, super-ego and id is more remindful of constitutional government, of evolution than of revolution.

While hypnosis and catharsis could be likened to explosion, to social revolution, psychoanalysis, based as it is now on reconstruction and restructuring, on interpretation of resistance and transference, and on the achieving of equilibrium between psychic forces, can be likened to constitutional government.

Of course, democratic constitutional government, the use of free election was then rather new in Central Europe, was untried and was distrusted but nevertheless gave rise to a new way of life, to new social experimentation in which violence was to be replaced by evolutionary processes. The people of the democratic state could no longer be compared with the seething cauldrons which are pictured in Le Bon's "Masses of the French Revolution" in his *Psychologie des Foules*. These people were now organized in political parties, into unions, into church groups and they worked on the problem of change, on the issues of compromise of social conflict by means of methods which were within the recognized due process of law.

A similar change has taken place in the psychoanalytic methods employed. One may wonder whether these parallels indicate that there is a direct relationship between psychotherapeutic methods employed and the social matrix out of which they grow. I do not claim a connection nor do I wish to see in the one a cause of the other. We might see mere incidental parallel processes, or we might be inclined to see such a connection. We may even be in danger to project into incidental manners of speaking quasi-insights.

Nevertheless it seems to be worth while to look for possible correlations between the development of psychoanalytic theory and technique and the changes in the social process. A case in point might be the different development of psychoanalysis in Europe and in the United States. In Europe until recently, as one can see from the published literature, psychoanalytic developments were comparatively little influenced by ego psychology, more and more dominant in American psychoanalytic literature. This is particularly interesting in view of the fact that American ego psychology was actually developed by former Europeans, who settled in the United States where the idea of government is expressed through the notion of checks and balances rather than those of revolution, chaos or counter-revolution through a dictatorship. Should it be mere chance that Hartmann's *Ego Psychology and the Problem of Adaptation*, actually published in 1939 in German, should have its tremendous impact on the evolution of psychoanalytic thought and technique in the United States? It is in this country, and societies with a similar way of life, that we speak about "conflict-free areas" in which all people can work together, that we speak about opportunities for solution of conflicts through arbitration, through means of checks and balances. Would it be surprising then that psychoanalytic theory and technique would be influenced by statements such as this:

> What is the structure of the external world to which the human organism adapts? At this point we cannot separate biological from social conceptions. I do not want to go into the possible analogies to the social life of animals. The first social relations of the child are crucial for the maintenance of his biological equilibrium also. It is for this reason that man's first object relations became our main concern in psychoanalysis. Thus the task of man to adapt to man is present from the very beginning of life. Furthermore, man adapts to an environment part of which has not, but part of which has already been molded by his kind and himself. Man not only adapts to the community but also actively participates in creating the conditions to which he must adapt. Man's environment is molded increasingly by man himself. Thus the crucial adaptation man has to make is to the social structure, and his collaboration in build-

191

ing it. This adaptation may be viewed in various of its aspects and from various points of view; here we are focusing on the fact that the structure of society, the process of division of labor, and the social locus of the individual co-determine the possibilities of adaptation and also regulate in part the elaboration of instinctual drives and the development of the ego. The structure of society decides (particularly—but not exclusively—through its effect on education) which forms of behavior shall have the greatest adaptive chance. . . . I discuss these familiar themes here merely to demonstrate the multiple layering of man's adaptation processes. In judging the degree of a person's adaptation —which is the implied basis of our concept of health— many factors must be taken into account, the concrete forms of which we are not yet familiar with.

These are the words of Hartmann and they highlight a new additional development in psychoanalysis as a theory and a therapeutic technique.

In Europe psychoanalysis has developed differently, as is indicated, for example, by the influence of Melanie Klein in England. It would also prove interesting how certain insights of psychoanalysis have been adopted by psychotherapeutic movements in Europe, and have been modified by and fused with notions from existential philosophy and literature related through the themes of military defeat, the dissolution of colonial empires, the problem of survival and naked existence.

Early social attempts to replace old, outmoded and oppressive structure through revolutions have here or there been replaced by attempts at social change through methods which make use of negotiation, of law and fuller participation of all members of society. Occasionally, as new societies emerge they return to older forms of social change. Might not one suggest that the same is true in the development of psychotherapy? Beginners frequently have to go through the whole process of the development of the science. The beginning analyst may see himself as someone who rescues patients, who must be tremendously powerful in order to pull patients out of their illness. He is tempted to use direct methods of a manipulative kind until he learns to see psychoanalysis as a collaborative process rather than as authoritarian manipulation of patients.

There is another parallel between the politician and the psychotherapist. Both are deeply involved with their method, seem to be immensely in love with it, and find it very difficult to part with the method, exchange the method as well as the ideology behind it, the theory behind it for a new one if indicated. It is for this reason that in the past psychoanalysts spoke about the psychoanalytic movement, a notion which was characteristic for the beginning struggles of the new science when it had to meet powerful opposition. This observation that the social scientists and clinicians find it difficult to have fruitful and rational discussions about their theories and techniques, that they are deeply and emotionally committed to their points of view, is of utmost importance if we are to face the difficulties in developing social and psychological sciences.

Freud has had the strength of character and a deep commitment to science which permitted him to give up certain aspects of psychoanalytic theory when they were no longer useful. He is a powerful counter-agent to the unhealthy overcommitment to theory and to method who was always ready to discard an outmoded notion for better insight. When he was seventy years old he gave up his earlier theory of anxiety. One would wish indeed that both social and psychological science would benefit from a view which Freud expressed in 1920: "We must be patient and await fresh methods and occasions of research. We must be ready too, to

193

abandon a path that we have followed for a time, if it seems to be leading to no good end. Only believers, who demand that science shall be a substitute for the catechism they have given up, will blame an investigator for developing or even transforming his views."

4.

The Psychotherapist's Own Values and His Role in the Handling of Value Problems

In Section 2, we discussed some of the value implications of different psychotherapeutic systems. These values determine firstly the *method* used, secondly the ideas about the *result* that is to be obtained.

With respect to the value characteristics of the *method*, the most outstanding differences seem to me the emphasis on the patient's ability to *think things through* with honesty and intellectual clarity, as against *authoritarian* and advisory *dictates* and as against involvement in *mystical or philosophical speculations*.

Among the value characteristics of the *results* to be obtained the generally most important seems to me the emphasis on the *freedom of choice which* Menninger, Kubie, May, Ekstein, and others put first.

Then, however, begin the variations. We mentioned in the Introduction C. Marshall Lowe's finding of four value orientations among therapists, which he called *naturalism, culturalism, humanism,* and *theism*. We found that they corresponded largely to preferences in the direction of one of the four basic tendencies I have postulated. The values would be to enable the patient primarily to find adequate satisfaction for his needs, to be socially adapted, to be creatively self-realizing, or else to be an integrated person with a philosophy of life.

Donald A. Bloch described as the prevailing goal of a large number of therapists to develop the patient to the kind of poise, control, and effectiveness as one might wish to find in a junior executive.

This ideal would fail to release in the patient the willingness to struggle for creative self-expression and it also would fail to open him up to a thoughtful integration of his existence into the general order of things in terms of philosophical or religious considerations.

There is up to now little clarification regarding these over-all orientations of psychotherapists and regarding their procedures in the direction of their ultimate goal.

The situation is just as confused if one asks how various concrete value problems, which come up during therapy, are being handled. The valuable book of Standal and Corsini (1959), *Critical Incidents in Psychotherapy*, deals with the manner in which various therapists proposed to handle them and gives the picture of a complete lack of unanimity in viewpoint and procedure.

Little has been done up to now to help the therapist in the clarification of this immensely complicated task: (1) He is left to his own devices in determining whether the values, value problems, and value conflicts of his patient are healthy or neurotic. (2) He must use his own judgment not only regarding the patient's insight potential but also regarding the factor which we called the patient's value potential and which determines the patient's eventual ability to apply the insight he acquired in action. (3) Furthermore, he must clarify the position he himself wants to take with respect to his patient's value system and value considerations. (4) Apart from this he must have come to terms with the values implied in the theory to which he suscribes and which may not in all respects correspond with his own feelings about things.

At the beginning of this volume I quoted examples of the varying positions taken by psychotherapists with respect to their own role in dealing with value problems. Different principles were described regarding the therapist's taking a stand or not when the patient discussed value problems. The problem of different culturally conditioned value systems of patient and therapist has been given a new kind of consideration by the various groups mentioned earlier. Different principles seem to obtain regarding the therapist's role when a patient appears to be incapable of *bringing values to materialization.*

With respect to this question, the general philosophy of most psychotherapists has been, under psychoanalytic influence, the assumption that anybody can be helped to an adequate adjustment provided he has sufficient insight ability.

Great pains have been taken to define, "that insight which is therapeutic" (Kubie, 1956, p. 122) and the "working through" by which it has to be followed, as against the therapeutically impotent insight.

But therapists increasingly come to the realization that even proper insight and working through do not enable all their patients to solve their problems and to become changed human beings.

At this point we may recall that Freud and some of his successors spoke—as mentioned before—of *postanalytic educational influences.* Freud spoke of "pressing the patient into a new decision," Alexander refers to, "an active influence of the analyst upon the assimilation process going on within the patient," Sterba speaks of a "formative activity of the analyst who must help the analysand to do something with the interpretation, that is, with the newly acquired knowledge about himself." He goes so far as to mention, "persuasion and threat, promise of reward, encouragement and praise," these means, he says, "are exactly those which we use in education in order to effect the shift from pleasure principle to reality principle." Sterba mentions quite a number of psychoanalysts who recognize "that pedagogic measures have their place in analytic therapy."

This earlier position taken by Freud and some of his immediate successors has been changed by a younger group who followed a certain technical model in using purely interpretative procedures.

Now we seem to find a renewed inclination in the direction of more active principles of therapy. But it seems to me we would make a mistake if we fell back into the formerly abandoned procedure of using the pressure of active measures without inquiring into what exactly we are doing and with whom.

The question of the function and impact of these postanalytic educational attempts was never really studied. The first thought that occurs is to ask why these attempts are called "postanalytic." Or one might say: Well maybe it is postanalytic, but is it altogether post-therapeutic? And even if it is postanalytic, how can this be left entirely to unpremeditated casualness, when up to now for years on end every move of the analyst was so carefully planned?

Furthermore, is it really as postanalytic as all that? Did we not hear that quite a number of analysts and other psychotherapists said they gave direct or indirect expression to personal opinions throughout the analysis? Thus, the values that they enhance in educational talks after analysis must have been in the picture all along during analysis.

There are many questions that these extraneous casual interventions arouse. Don't they, if they are actual suggestions, possibly induce new repressions if the patient tries to please his therapist? Furthermore, don't they if not presented in terms of alternative solutions of life, but as suggestions instead, impair the patient's freedom of decision? Lastly, why should these interventions be necessary at all? This leads back to the finding that insight alone does not guarantee a cure. So little does it, that Alexander (1956) can say, "The most confusing and even discouraging fact in our field is the unpredictability of therapeutic results. . . ." (p. 84).

We explained this in a previous section with the fact that the insight potential of a patient and his value potential are not the same. His value potential, both in terms of the values he can truly identify with and those he can bring to materialization, needs to be evaluated by the therapist. This may not always be possible before therapy since we do not yet possess diagnostic means to evaluate values. But it is probably possible after a short period of exploratory work.

A case in point was reported during the meetings of the previously mentioned Los Angeles Value Study Group by Alvin A. Lasko:

> The case was that of a professional gambler who came to Lasko with the problem of impotence. When informed about the methods by which this man made his living, Lasko doubted whether his own ethical code permitted him to treat a person who made his living by consciously taking advantage of people.
>
> As a believer in self-realization as the goal of life and of therapy, he felt he might help a basically dishonest person to more effective application of his dishonesty.

198

But in studying the case somewhat longer, he discovered that this man lived only peripherally both in his work and in his life; that he had no relationships with people and could not perform in anything where he had to deal with people; that his impotence was an expression of his own low self-value.

It transpired also that the man knew what he was doing, but that up to now he had not been able to face it and to face himself.

Lasko judged that Mr. X had adequate insight ability and enough ego strength to face and to cope with his problem and to restructure his personality as well as his life.

The conviction with which Lasko continued to work on this case, was justified by his patient's continuous development.

Lasko obviously performed what we have called the evaluation of the patient's value potential. In this procedure he brought his own personal standards as well as his theoretical value concepts to bear on the case.

This then raises the second question. Can we find any *general principles* and *specific rules* according to which the *therapist* should bring *his own convictions* into the picture.

As far as the therapist's personal standards are concerned, this is an ethical question. The therapist's integrity requires that he maintain his own standards. This was brought out in Lasko's case.

Ginsburg and Herma (1953) formulate it in a previously quoted passage:

> The analyst who feels strongly motivated by social values cannot turn aside from such activities without undermining his own integrity and feeling of self-esteem and any such denial might well affect his relationship with his patients, certainly as much and more so than mere compliance with a technical rule (p. 558).

199

There are however situations where the patient's welfare is endangered by the therapist's taking a stand that is much at variance from the patient's. An example from the author's case material may be quoted briefly.

Katharine is a thirty-nine-year-old, married woman who was referred for the treatment of a severe obsessive-compulsive neurosis with strong paranoid and schizoid tendencies. In fact she had had a psychotic break soon after some traumatic experiences connected with her marriage and her immigration. At that time she received shock treatments in an eastern state hospital.

She was an immigrant from a European country and referred by an American psychiatrist who felt that in her case the similar cultural background of the therapist might be of the essence. In this he was correct, as Katharine was to an unusual degree more embedded in her European past than in her American present.

Among the many unresolved childhood conflicts from which she suffered, the problem of her *identification* stood out as one of the most disturbing.

Her parents came from extremely different backgrounds, socioeconomically as well as in their religion. Her mother was a Catholic, her father a Protestant, and while the child was raised as a Protestant, at the insistance of the father, for quite a while the mother secretly took her to Mass in a Catholic Church. The child was also present at parental arguments during which she heard her mother lament about Hell and Damnation to which Katharine might be condemned. She felt terrible anxiety concerning Hell for herself and for her mother.

Also, the father's concept of the demands of religion was very strict and Katharine grew up full of fears and anxiety with regard to the religious threats her parents made. While at the time she of course did not know that her mother was a severely depressed hypochondriac and her father a physically very sick man, she obviously felt that both her parents were endangered by death. These fears were further enhanced by a paternal grandmother and a maternal aunt who talked in this vein.

Katharine did not know what to believe and with whom to identify. She disliked both religions, but she did not dare, admit this to herself till very much later. Religion was one of the most fearful obstacles to her identification.

Probably, she would have found it easier to identify with one of the two religions, if she had been able to identify wholeheartedly with one of her parents. This, however, was also not possible for her. Her feelings about both her parents were mixed. She did not admire her mother, who was given to complaining and nagging and who from the beginning was very demanding of the child. Also Katharine felt that her mother neglected her due to her excessive preoccupation with her own problems. In other words, she did not really feel loved by her mother. She originally idolized her father and felt loved by him. But her relationship with him was soon spoiled because he was not a well man and, besides being a disciplinarian, he had spells of irritation and of rage. In such moments, he might beat the child mercilessly for comparatively small misdemeanors.

Katharine, who was never close to anybody, did not consider closeness when she fell in love with and married a man who again came from a socioeconomic, religious, and cultural background completely different from her own. Her attempts at identifying with him and his mental world failed, because she had in the meantime developed some philosophy of her own.

With this man, she moved to America and met with a culture that was entirely foreign to her and to which she felt highly antagonistic; this resulted in her breakdown.

It is clear for this woman it was necessary, more than anything else, that her therapist should be entirely and totally *for* her. This put her present, as it had put her previous, therapist into a very difficult position. Katharine's views were hostile to the American democratic philosophy of life and hostile to any kind of religion. They evolved from very

201

outdated imperialistic, feudalistic, class-discriminating, and frankly selfish principles by which she believed she would benefit. The present, as well as the previous, therapist realized the identification problem of this woman and initially tried to ignore her whole mental superstructure, to lead the patient back to her basic emotional problems in relationship with her parents as persons.

While, under the circumstances, no stand was taken by either therapist, the patient was quite aware of the fact that no enthusiastic agreement with her ideas was forthcoming from her therapists.

For a while she allowed herself to be brought back to the fundamental emotional dynamics of her relationship with her parents. Apart from intermittent political and philosophical outbursts, she worked very consistently and with increasing insight through the early conflicts of her love-hate relationship with both her father and mother.

But when, after several years, she had reached a certain platform of equanimity, lessened anxiety, and decreased symptoms, she returned with renewed vigor to the discussion of her philosophy and she declared with some awareness that anyone who was not for her philosophy was not for *her*, and it was quite clear to her that the therapist probably had a completely different philosophy, "one of those silly idealistic and social philanthropic views." When challenged outright in this way, the therapist eventually agreed that her orientation was different whereupon a regressive period full of anxieties, suicide ideas, and hostility against the therapist set in.

After that, the patient marked time till she took up the subject again. This time the therapist tried a different approach. She attempted to find a platform on which, in spite of different views, an identification remained possible. First, following the suggestion of a colleague, she tried to underemphasize the importance of different views. More important than views was the personal relationship, since views can change and are perhaps not so completely different from one another. This the patient rejected emphatically. She ardently emphasized that she believed only in what was good for herself, and that was the opposite of the therapist's foolish philanthropy.

At this point the therapist reaffirmed her stand but added that she felt that they were both honestly striving to find answers to the problem of life; they had this honest striving in common. The patient seemed to feel less rejected, but she was slightly suspicious regarding this approach to their difference. So she declared she had to think things over. And this is where the matter has stood for several months.

Let us see exactly what happened here. First of all, both the colleagues I consulted and I myself were obviously appraising two things: one, the patient's needs, and secondly, the patient's value potential. The patient's needs were apparently still as they always had been, to have the therapist completely for and with her.

In transferring her fears for her mother's life to the therapist, she cannot let the therapist die as long as the therapist had still all these wrong beliefs. She had not yet changed in her death fears for herself and her mother substitute.

But since both were honestly striving, neither she nor her therapist were lost. She began to be able to accept this. She had improved to the point of recognizing and understanding her needs and recognizing her illness as due to the fact that her needs had never been met. This recognition made things easier for her. At times she could joke about her compulsiveness. Also, the shift from religion to politics indicates that the feeling of danger has lessened; it is not really condemnation to Hell any more that threatens: death still may threaten.

There is more. The real source of her recent strength came from something aside from her recognition of her needs and her understanding of her past. In working through the experiences of her past, she had reached certain conclusions. She felt that her parents had never given genuine consideration to her needs, but that they had always pursued their own needs and turned them into duties for her. She had decided that she had a right to her own needs, just as her parents did. She decided furthermore that there was no objective criterion for what was better or worse and that actually everybody's opinions were serving only the individual's needs. After clarifying this for herself, Katharine wanted the therapist to assume the same position that she had assumed politically and religiously, rather than that she should be made to identify with the therapist's "silly idealism."

Katharine had worked out her philosophy gradually and with great circumspection. For a while she had made a number of small attempts to accomplish certain things beyond her own need-satisfaction. She forced herself to cultivate more social relationships for her husband and her son, she cooked special things, and she tried to raise orchids for sale both as a creative activity and to increase the family income. But sooner or later she dropped these attempts and limited herself to the necessities of household work. "All I want," she said when discussing the disturbance she experienced when she tried to pursue such far-reaching goals, "is to have peace."

This then seems a case in point of a limited value potential. The patient resigns herself to pursuing exclusively need-satisfying and order-upholding tendencies ("to have peace"). That is to say, she limits herself to goals of maintenance and to doing a minimum in the direction of adaptive or creative changing.

At this point in the therapy it did not seem that much could be done, at least for the time being, about her limited value potential. Consequently, the therapist tried to accept it and to do what seemed most *constructive* under the cir-

204

cumstances. And by "constructive" we mean the relative best the patient was able to achieve in coping with her given conditions of life without actually damaging herself and her environment.

The limited value potential of this patient determined the philosophy of life she chose. In her case the therapist concurred with her choice of a philosophy of life that seemed to help her sustain and improve her mental health. This patient at least for the time being was obviously not able to work toward self-realization or any fulfillment beyond the maintenance of her equilibrium.

5.

Discussion by James S. Simkin

The following two cases demonstrate two situations in which the therapist shares and does not share his own values with patients.

The first case is one in which the therapist felt it necessary to express his own value judgments. The second case illustrates the opposite position.

Mortimer, a seventeen-year old only child whose primary symptom is stuttering, and who had been encouraged by me to express his suppressed anger, described with great glee that he had spotted his sixty-six-year-old father driving in the city one evening when he purportedly was out of town on business. Furthermore, the patient was almost certain that there was a woman (not his mother) in the car with "the old man." He told me that he planned to confront his father directly with his newly acquired knowledge, in order to let him know that he is aware of his playing around, and to blackmail the father into paying more attention to him.

205

In addition, Mortimer was convinced this action would result in his father beginning to treat him (the patient) more like an adult!

Now, from my own value orientation, blackmail is personally repugnant to me, even if it worked! My decision in that particular value situation was to directly express to Mortimer my own feelings about blackmail as well as to explore with him the possible repercussions to this act. I indicated that in my judgment blackmail was always immature behavior and even if it did succeed in "making the old boy aware" of him, it could never succeed in getting someone to judge him as an adult. His counter-argument was that in his world adults frequently used blackmailing techniques to win their point! We ended the hour by my indicating to him that I was one adult who would not reinforce this (distorted?) perception of all adults—that I wanted him to know how I felt about blackmail—but that I respected his right to judge for himself how he would use the information about his father—if at all.

It is important to note that Mortimer's environment is heavily influenced by his parents. They determine to a large extent whom he may associate with, how late he may stay out, and so forth, and he is still completely dependent on them financially. He does not have as great an opportunity to explore the world and arrive at his own value system as does Charles.

Charles, a twenty-two-year-old construction worker has been in therapy two years. His primary symptom, too, was stuttering, and he had had some additional two years of work at the speech clinic of one of the major Universities in the Los Angeles area. The head of the clinic made the referral indicating that Charles probably required intensive psychotherapy. Many characterological problems had been evidenced and very little progress made with the stuttering. At the clinic he had maintained a rather supercilious attitude, had attempted to date one of the female staff workers, and had in other ways demonstrated what was considered immature judgment and behavior.

Psychological testing revealed an immature, passive-dependent, oral character who was above average in intelligence (IQ-112), with considerable evidence of unbridled impulsiveness and tendencies to act out feelings. A psychiatric evaluation at the beginning of treatment indicated: "psychoneurosis, anxiety reaction in a passive dependent individual who early in life had suffered a great loss of self-esteem. His reaction formation takes the shape of 'being one of the guys,' being a tough guy, demonstrating a violent temper. He has been only superficially successful and is essentially lonesome and fearful."

From the very beginning of our work together he has, as of this writing, been seen for some 235 hours, marked differences in value orientation between the patient and myself became apparent. One of the earliest concerned his attitudes toward traffic laws. From his point of view, red lights, when no cars were visible (especially police cars) were to be run through; stop-signs ignored; speed limits exceeded, etc. These rules were made to be broken and the only crime involved was getting caught. (From my own value orientation, which I did *not* share with him, I perceive these rules not as infringements on my own individual freedom or as challenges to my ingenuity, but as necessary to control traffic and safeguard human lives.) However, despite Charles' cautiousness in regard to making sure there were no police in evidence when he broke traffic rules, he managed to systematically collect traffic violations to the point where he was obviously jeopardizing his privilege of driving, and our work focused on the underlying self-punishment evidenced.

Another value situation presented itself in terms of payment of fees. Since the beginning of treatment and until very recently, Charles has not paid his fees regularly, on time, or in full. As this trend became apparent, I brought it up and discovered that Charles had left a trail of debts cross-country. He was especially "angry" as he put it, when he would get a bill from a professional person such as a dentist or a physician, for service, and either made partial payments or none at all. He had also, over a period of time, borrowed sums of money from his father, also a construction worker, with whom he had lived both in the east and south-west, and who currently lived in Los Angeles but not with the patient.

My own personal attitude toward debts is quite different, and I place great value on paying my bills promptly. In this situation again I did not discuss my own values, but focussed rather on the psychodynamics of his behavior. I did not feel it appropriate to juxtapose my own value orientation because of three counts: (1) The "meaning" of with-holding payment from authority figures I think, is dynamically clear and the transference elements in this behavior a veritable goldmine for analysis; (2) my own compulsive need to pay promptly is neurotically motivated; and (3) unlike Mortimer, Charles' reality situation is not complicated by any economic dependence on his parents.

Under no circumstance do I consciously attempt to direct or persuade the patient to adopt my values since I am convinced that values are functional, relative and idiosyncratic, rather than organic, absolute and generalized. What is meaningful and valuable to me need not and frequently is not meaningful or valuable to someone else.

Why then did I share my values in one situation directly with Mortimer and not with Charles? It is my belief that one of the primary functions, if not *the* primary function of psychotherapy is to teach patients to *discriminate*. Not in the popular negative sense as in racial or religious discrimination, but in the natural organismic sense of picking and choosing what is appropriate, what does something for them. In my judgment, Mortimer's environment is so restricted by his parents it is necessary for me to *directly* expose him to other possibilities in the area of value judgments. With Charles, on the other hand, it is not necessary to *complicate* the therapy (I see no other choice in dealing with adolescents) by injecting my own value judgments. Charles lives in a much broader world than Mortimer. He *is* exposed to many value systems. If he does not "see" we can analyze his scotomatization. If he chooses not to adopt a particular value after "seeing" it, then that value is *not* appropriate for him.

Certainly identification, transference, introjection, and the like are ongoing processes in both cases, or for that matter in *all* cases. These phenomena are all great for the therapeutic will. In my opinion, psychotherapy is a learning process. The therapist must judge what will help facilitate learning in each specific case. I believe it is necessary to share values with patients whose environment is so restricted (be it by parents or severe psychopathology, or whatever) that they are crippled in making choices.

6.
The Problem of Introducing a Philosophy of Life

What is the therapist's role with respect to the patient's *philosophy of life* when a good value potential exists? This question leads to a problem of great consequence.

There is no standardized philosophy of life and in all likelihood there never will be. Even within the pattern of common trends within one culture, there is still a great variety of outlooks on life and its purpose. The patient is in one way or another influenced by his therapist's philosophy of life, whether both acknowledge this fact or not.

Beyond the inculcation that takes place in this way, there are therapists who will, as we discussed above, introduce their own philosophy of life not only when challenged, as was the case with Katharine, but as a spontaneous expression of their own conviction.

As far as I could gather from sources available to me, there seem to be various considerations underlying interventions by various therapists. One consideration is that in the therapists' judgment the patient must at this moment be given a *new direction in life* because his progress is presently hampered by his inability to get himself out of a certain thought pattern or to give himself a new direction.

> An example in point is an intervention made by a colleague who permitted me this quotation. The incident concerned a patient, Betty, who was given to a great deal of worry with respect to problems that concerned her family's and husband's future more than their actual everyday life.
> Her therapist intervened with the question of why she felt she had to worry so much about the future, could she not try to take each day as it came along without concerning herself constantly with the future. He supported his suggestion by some ideas of existential philosophy.

The reason this therapist gave for his intervention was that he wanted to give the patient a new direction. He thought giving her this new philosophy might stimulate her to change her behavior, even though the underlying problems were not resolved. Other therapists might have preferred quite different approaches to the problem of worrying than the teaching of existentialistic or any other philosophy. In fact, they might judge the introduction of new ideas premature at this point, and they might feel the patient should simply have been made to explore the dynamics and origin of her worrying, which she could undoubtedly recognize as an inappropriate procedure.

If the first criterion for the introduction of new ideas to the patient is the consideration that at a certain *time* specific efforts have to be made to help the patient abandon his continued pursuit of certain thought or behavior patterns, it should be possible to clarify and exemplify the handling of this criterion.

When the introduction of new ideas actually seems indicated, it might be considered desirable to open up several possible new concepts to a patient instead of indoctrinating him with just one philosophy or one dogma.

My own approach is to ask at a certain advanced stage, in what I have called (1953) the fourth phase of therapy, at an appropriate moment: "What exactly are you living for?" or, "Do you think you have a goal of life?" The answer one gets may vary from such acknowledgments of the unresolved problem as "I wish I knew," or "That is a good question," to refutations such as "Oh, I think it will take time to find this out," or to the statement of definite convictions, such as "Oh, I think I just want to make my husband and my family happy, and now I hope I will gradually be able to do this much better than before," or "I know I need a definite purpose in life and now I think I want to begin to explore this more concretely." Some will also say: "I wish I would understand better than I do what life and the world are about. I don't know—my religion has not satisfied me for a long time, yet there must be something, some supreme being, otherwise, how could it all have started?"

Depending on these measures, I will try to help the patient think through various possible solutions of the question of a point of view.

A case in which the factor of *age roles* in life and the idea of the life cycle was introduced by me at a comparatively early stage was the following.

> Diane, thirty-four-years old who as she said, had started her life as a "career girl"—she had taught art at a local college—had recently married and did not feel happy about her decision. Although presumably very fond of the man, who was divorced and several years her senior, she found that apart from a problem of sexual incompatibility, their interests ran too far apart—he was an accountant—and that as personalities, they did not jibe as well as was hoped for by both.
>
> The man, Ed, who was very much in love with Diane, wanted to do everything to work their problem out, while she considered divorce. But her fondness and respect for Ed as well as questions of conscience brought her into therapy after unsuccessful marriage counseling.

From the start, it was obvious that this case was full of complexities. There was the probability of a latent homosexual trend along with many other problems in the sex area, such as an early trauma; there was a mother who lived a dreary existence and seemed happy neither as a wife nor as a mother; there was a family clan who felt, women should marry and not concern themselves with careers; there were glamorous and inspiring women whose example made a career life seem preferable and incompatible with marriage and so on.

While it was evident that this would be a long trek in

which the exploratory work would be drawn out by much resistance, I felt that in view of the distressing situation in which both marital partners were suffering, everything possible should be done to get the therapy going.

For this reason, I used an occasion that arose at a fairly early stage, after a few months, to introduce the factor "time" as follows:

I had asked Diane before why she had married at all, since she had planned to be an unmarried career woman. Her answer the first time was vague—she had thought Ed was such a good man, he loved her so, maybe this was a good idea after all, and so on. This time, when I asked again, why exactly had she married at all? she said: "Well in the long run I thought the other would not work out as well."

"Why?"

"Well, I thought maybe people should marry, it gets so lonely after a while."

"Had you ever thought of wanting children?"

"Yes, naturally I want a family, that is one of the reasons for marriage, did I not say that? Only I was not yet really ready for that at all."

Then I asked: "Did you ever consider age factors?"

"Age factors? What do you mean?" She became somewhat confused. "Do you mean, I am perhaps getting a little old to start a family? Frankly, I have never really thought about age—there were so many other problems to think about. . . ."

"Well," I said, "I had really thought that when you finally decided to marry, age was somehow in your mind.

"Somehow, I suppose."

"You said you were not yet ready to think about children. Suppose you decide to divorce and to find another partner, as you said you might want to—it might of course get rather late."

"Well of course, now that you say it, I can see, I must have

213

thought of age without knowing it—I have never thought it through. It seems ridiculous now since you say it. . . ."

We discussed briefly the curve of life and the various age potentials, and while of course this did not touch nor change the fundamental conflict situation, it served as a spur and incentive for harder work on the side of a patient who up to then had handled her problem without any other consideration that that of her own acute feelings. It naturally served not as a motive, but as a frame of reference, which this intelligent woman had, strangely enough, disregarded or wanted to forget.

The introduction of the consideration of the age factor in this case was chosen as an intermediary step between two extremes: one would have been letting the patient go on in her oblivion disregarding anything except her own acute emotional disturbance; the other would have been an actual reminder of other factors in the situation, such as the pressure under which she put her husband and the forgetfulness that she permitted herself regarding the disadvantage under which she would put the family she wanted to have if she deferred much longer starting it.

The introduction of the time consideration in this case might be subsumed under what Schmideberg (1961) calls "linking *incentives* to the patient's preoccupation." Her own example is not dissimilar. She says: "In the second interview, I told a woman in her forties who was worried by her 'hot flashes' that satisfactory sex life is likely to diminish them, and this made her resume sexual relations with her husband" (p. 256).

I call the procedure with which I am experimenting *"constructive exploration."* This procedure is being carefully utilized in the process of the patient's extrication from the obstructive forces, as was shown in the case of Diane. Later it is used to assist the patient in building up his new value system. In doing this, giving direction is avoided. For the most part, the patient is made aware of considerations that he himself was making implicitly.

The recognition of the fact that we need to get more comparative information about the possible ways of handling not only the problems of our patients but also their values, has led to the publication of an enlightening and valuable volume, *Critical Incidents in Psychotherapy,* edited by S. W. Standal and R. J. Corsini (1959).

In this book, twenty-three critical incidents in psychotherapy are reported anonymously and twenty-eight other therapists comment on the handling of selected incidents. The original report as well as the comments give a good idea of the great variety of theoretical principles by which different therapists are guided in their handling of certain types of problems.

In a case of imprudent acting-out behavior (case seventeen), for example, many different opinions were stated about the wisdom of taking an authoritarian role, of being supportive-permissive too long, of failing to introduce new values, of failing to have a more positive program, of abusing the therapeutic role by threats, and so on.

In another case of sexual promiscuity (case two), there was a general agreement about the appropriateness of occasional authoritarian treatment. I myself found an authoritarian approach in two cases of extreme promiscuity entirely unsuccessful.

There were different opinions regarding an active intervention in a suicide case (case eight).

"The appropriate value orientation for the role of the

therapist" is discussed by Ackerman and Riesman. The article suggests the importance of further studies of incidents concerning complex valuational choices.

7.
Research Problems on Values in Psychotherapy

In concluding our survey, we find that there appear to be five main situations that might arise and prompt an intervention from those therapists who feel they have an active function in the patient's orientation toward values. Briefly stated, they are the following:

1. The first situation may arise when a patient has seemingly successfully worked through his problems and when he should begin to bring acknowledged new values to materialization.

This is the historically familiar situation to which Freud and some of his immediate successors reacted with a type of *pressuring* that we characterized at the beginning of this volume. Actually, the psychoanalytic theory implies that if a person has worked through his problems sufficiently and has acquired adequate insight, things should fall into place and no effort on the part of the therapist should be necessary to activate new behavior patterns. They would come about gradually and without anybody's pushing. We all have, of course, perhaps even as the bulk of our practices, this most gratifying type of case.

When we meet with the other type of case in which new behavior patterns do not set in as automatically as we hoped they would, two possibilities must be considered. One is that the case was not treated long enough or not analyzed on a sufficiently deep level. This is the usual psychoanalytic assumption. Freud, Sterba, and some other analysts assumed, however, that even in sufficiently analyzed cases there was sometimes a sluggishness or reticence to effect changes.

Schmideberg (1961) expresses the opinion that too long a continuation of motivational exploration can at times be detrimental and prevent the patient from developing effective incentives.

> The danger of stressing insight, unconscious motivation, and the past, is that it often distracts the patient and even the therapist from concentrating on realistic consequences, on purpose, and the future. Some patients are only too ready to use motivational "insight" as an excuse for not acting. Often free associations into causes are nothing but the ruminations, grievances, and self-accusations of the neurotic or depressed; to encourage them only makes the patient more abnormal and inactive (p. 257).

The question of what to do instead of further analysis of a case is answered by Schmideberg with the frank suggestion of a *guiding* or *pressuring* approach, such as Freud himself has recommended.

The problems that this suggestion brings up, were discussed at length in our introductory chapter.

A second possibility is that in this unsuccessful group we may find those patients whose value potential was overestimated from the start and who are actually not capable of extending themselves any further. An example was the case of Ben.

Where does this leave us? Are these the cases that we have to give up when we reach an impasse that cannot be overcome? This, I think, should be faced realistically and studied through actual case material.

2. A second situation in which the therapist may face a problem with respect to the patient's value orientation, was brought up by Ginsburg and Herma. They point out that there are situations in which the analyst would undermine his own *integrity* and *feeling of self-esteem* if he avoided taking a stand in certain matters that concern the welfare of mankind and of society.

A case in point was Lasko's gambler, whom he felt he could treat only if he could hope to change the man's value system. Simkin's case discussion refers to this situation and his different handling of it in two different situations.

This type of case might under certain circumstances bring up irresolvable *identity* conflicts. Ginsburg, several discussants of his paper, Wolberg, Sterba, Frankl, and others emphasize that the therapist should not impose his value system but help the patient find his own. This, however, is often much more complicated than it appears.

First, it is much easier said than done, *not to influence* a patient. Certain types of patients are forever reacting to the therapist as an authority who should know the answer. Other patients—an example was given in the case of Katharine—feel rejected and shaken in their security if the therapist does not seem to agree with their values. The therapist's position that everybody has a right to his own outlook on life, is experienced as nonsupportive.

In a further group of cases, the *cultural discrepancy* between patient and therapist affects communication and identification, particularly in the area of values. This became evident in such studies as those by Redlich and Bingham

(1953), Marvin K. Opler (1956), in *Explorations in Social Psychiatry*, edited by A. H. Leighton, J. A. Clausen, and R. N. Wilson (1957), in the studies of John P. Spiegel and his group (1959), and others.

3. A third situation in which a therapist may feel impelled or even compelled to *intervene* would be one in which a *change of direction* of the patient's goals or behavior seem acutely indicated..

Examples in point are offered in the interesting book edited by Standal and Corsini, *Critical Incidents in Psychotherapy*, which we discussed above.

It is important to note that some of the critics feel certain critical incidents need not have arisen if the case had been handled differently from the beginning. But probably there still remain cases of actual critical incidents and of most desirable changes of direction that may demand actions on the therapist's part.

A variation of an actual intervention meant to effect a change of direction would be the introduction of a *new parameter* for the patient's consideration, as was demonstrated in the case of Diane. The therapist's referral to the aspect of age gave the patient a new frame of reference for her orientation. From this reorientation the patient might eventually derive a new *incentive* without this having been actually prompted by the therapist.

4. A fourth situation, which induces some psychotherapists to encourage and assist their patients with certain decisions, may arise in connection with choices that have to be made.

Questions of choice present themselves frequently of course. Bela Mittelman mentions in his discussion of Ginsburg's and Herma's paper his helping and even directing a patient with the decision of a change from one occupation to another.

Choices with respect to duty conflicts may occur, and as Allan Wheelis says, the patient may implore the analyst to provide him with value criteria, which the fluctuating value system of our culture no longer provides. The case of Georgia was an example in point. The therapist might in such cases structure for the patient the changes in value orientation that are taking place and can advise him regarding different possible solutions among which he might choose.

Decisions about a possible new course of action may induce a therapist to point out a completely new possibility that he feels the patient would not see himself. He may feel that *lack of resourcefulness* due to lack of information or lack of imagination may prevent a patient from seeing all possibilities open to him.

In this situation, there are of course many pitfalls to be considered. One lies in the question of whether or not the patient has acquired enough *inner freedom* to follow the newly suggested course of action.

The second danger is that the *therapist's own thinking* may be one-sided, and may reflect a point of view with which others could not agree at all. The question is then, what right does he have to pass on his prejudices to others?

5. This leads, then, to the fifth situation, which is bound to arise specifically in our work with children and adolescents or younger and inexperienced people, a situation where a therapist switches knowingly or unknowingly to the role of *educator*. In other words, he finds himself in the situation where he has *to introduce and to emphasize values* that the less mature person has not as yet conceived. This has been

discussed by Fromm-Reichmann (1950), who, particularly in her work with schizophrenics actually speaks of guidance to more adequate values: it is also brought out repeatedly by various commentators on the cases in the Standal-Corsini (1959) volume.

The problem here is again a question of what right the therapist has to become an educator and to encourage values as he sees them. Particularly problematic is the situation when we deal with adolescents whose parents in our opinion have failed to enhance the right sort of values for their children. A case in point was presented by J. S. Simkin (see the discussion of Mortimer, pp. 205 ff.).

These fourth and fifth points of our methodological discussion lead into the question of the relationship of psychotherapy to education.

In enumerating five frequent and typical situations that might involve a therapist in the value problems and conflicts of his patients, I do not claim completeness. I bring examples, not a system.

I also do not claim to have answers, I merely raise questions. Comprehensive studies of a larger group of therapists from different schools will be required to state principles that after sufficient experimentation might become more generally acceptable.

References

Ach, N. Über die Willenstätigkeit und das Denken (About Will and Thinking). In D. Rapaport (Ed.), *Organization and Pathology of Thought.* New York: Columbia University Press, 1951. Pp. 15–38.

Ackerman, N. W. Goals in Therapy. Round Table Discussion. *Amer. J. Psychoanalys.*, 1956, 16(1), 3–4.

Alexander, F. Discussion of "Aims and Limitations of Psychotherapy" by P. H. Hoch. In F. Fromm-Reichmann and J. L. Moreno (Eds.), *Progress in Psychotherapy.* New York: Grune & Stratton, 1956.

———. Unexplored Areas in Psychoanalytic Theory. *Behavioral Sci.*, 1958, 3, 293–316.

———, and T. M. French. *Psychoanalytic Therapy.* New York: Ronald, 1946.

Alexander, I. E., and A. M. Adlerstein. Death and Religion. In H. Feifel (Ed.), *The Meaning of Death.* New York: McGraw-Hill, 1959.

Allport, G. The Use of Personal Documents in Psychological Science. *Soc. Sci. Research Council,* 1942.

———. The Trend in Motivational Theory. In C. E. Moustakas (Ed.), *The Self, Explorations in Personal Growth.* New York: Harper, 1956.

Arendt, H. *The Human Condition.* Chicago: University of Chicago Press, 1951.

223

Baldwin, J. M. *History of Psychology*. New York: Putnam, 1913.

Bender, L., and A. Freedman. A Study of the First Three Years in the Maturation of Schizophrenic Children. *Quart. J. Child Behav.*, 1952, 4.

——. When the Childhood Schizophrenic Grows Up. *Amer. J. Orthopsychiat.*, 1957, 27(3), 553–565.

Bergman, P. The Role of Faith in Psychotherapy. *Bull. Menninger Clin.*, 1958, 22.

Bertalanffy, L. V. Human Values in a Changing World. In A. H. Maslow (Ed.), *New Knowledge in Human Values*. New York: Harper, 1959.

Binswanger, L. The Case of Ellen West. In R. May, E. Angel, and H. F. Ellenberger (Eds.), *Existence*. New York: Basic Books, 1958.

Bloch, D. A. Values, Psychoanalytic and Otherwise. In J. H. Masserman (Ed.), *Psychoanalysis and Human Values*. New York: Grune & Stratton, 1960.

Bolgar, Hedda. *The Role of Values in the Psychotherapeutic Process*. (In preparation.)

Bowlby, J. *Maternal Care and Mental Health*. World Health Organization Monograph, Geneva, Switzerland, 1953.

Brinton, C. *The Shaping of the Modern Mind*. New York: New American Library, 1953. Pp. 11–12.

Brody, S. *Patterns of Mothering*. New York: International Universities Press, 1956.

Bronfenbrenner, U. The Study of Identification through Interpersonal Perception. In *Person Perception and Interpersonal Behavior*. Stanford, California: Stanford University Press, 1958. Pp. 110–130.

Bugental, J. F., and S. L. Zelen. Investigations into the "Self-Concept." *J. Personal.*, 1950, 18, 483–498.

Buhler, Charlotte. *The First Year of Life*. New York: John Day, 1930.

——. Drei Generationen im Tagebuch (Three Generations in Diaries). *Qu. u. Stud. z. Jgdkde.*, 1934, 2, pp. 1–184.

——. The Reality Principle. *Amer. J. Psychother.*, 1954, 4, 626–647.

——. Earliest Trends in Goal-Setting. *Rev. de Psychiat. Infant.*, 1958, 25(1–2), 13–23.

——. Der menschliche Lebenslauf als psychologisches Problem

(The Human Course of Life as a Psychological Problem). Göttingen, Germany: Verlag. f. Psych., 1959.

———. Gemeinsame Grundzüge und Probleme moderner Psychotherapie (Common Trends and Problems of Modern Psychotherapy). In Anniversary Volume for Karl Buhler, *J. f. exper. u. angew. Psycho.*, 1959, 6(1).

———. Theoretical Observations about Life's Basic Tendencies. *Amer. J. Psychother.*, 1959, 13(3), 501–581.

———. Werte in der Psychotherapie (Values in Psychotherapy). In V. E. Frankl, V. E. v. Gebsattel, and J. H. Schultz (Eds.), *Handb. d. Neurosenlehre u. Psychother.* Munich: Urban & Schwarzenberg, 1960. Vol. 5, pp. 588–604.

———. Meaningful Living in the Mature Years. In R. W. Kleemeier (Ed.), *Aging and Leisure.* New York: Oxford University Press, 1961.

———. Genetic Aspects of the Self. *Mon. N.Y. Acad. Sciences.* 1962.

———. The Infant's First Reactions to the Other Human Being. *J. Soc. Psychiat.* (In press.)

———, H. Hetzer, and B. Tudor-Hart. Soziologische und psychologische Studien über das erste Lebensjahr (Sociological and Psychological Studies about the First Year of Life). *Qu. u. Stud. z. Jgdkde*, 1927, 5.

Buhler, K. *Die Krise der Psychologie* (The Crisis of Psychology). Jena: G. Fischer, 1929.

———. *Sprachtheorie* (Theory of Language). Jena: G. Fischer, 1934.

Cleveland, E. J., and W. D. Longaker. Neurotic Patterns in the Family. In A. H. Leighton, J. A. Clausen, and R. N. Wilson (Eds.), *Explorations in Social Psychiatry.* New York: Basic Books, 1957.

Colby, K. M. *Energy and Structure in Psychoanalysis.* New York: Ronald, 1955.

Danzinger, L., and L. Frankl. Zum Problem der Funktionsreifung (About the Problem of Functional Maturation). *Z. Kinderforschung*, 1934, 43, 219–254.

Diethelm, O. Goals in Therapy. Round Table Discussion. *Amer. J. Psychoanal.*, 1956, 12(1), 3–4.

Eiduson, B. T. Brain Mechanisms and Psychotherapy. *Amer. J. Psychiat.*, 1958, 115(3), 203–210.

Eiduson, B. T., S. Eiduson, and E. Geller. Biochemistry, Genetics and the Nature-Nurture Problem. *Amer. J. Orthopsychiat.* (In press.)

Ekstein, R. Structural Aspects of Psychotherapy. *Psychoanalytic Review*, 1952, 39, 222–228.

———. Psychoanalytic Techniques. In *Progress in Clinical Psychology*, Vol. 5. New York: Grune & Stratton. Pp. 79–97.

———. Faith and Reason in Psychotherapy. *Bull. Menninger Clin.*, 1958, 22.

———. On the Nature of the Psychotherapeutic Process. *Bull. Veterans Administration*, October, 1957, 3–12.

Erikson, E. H. *Childhood and Society.* New York: Norton, 1950.

———. *Identity and the Life Cycle.* New York: International Universities Press, 1959.

Escalona, S., and G. M. Heider. *Prediction and Outcome.* New York: Basic Books, 1959.

———., and M. Leitch. Early Phases of Personality Development: A Non-Normative Study of Infant Behavior. *Mon. Soc. Research in Child Devel.*, 1953, 17(54), 1.

Feifel, H. Attitudes toward Death in some Normal and Mentally Ill Populations. In H. Feifel (Ed.), *The Meaning of Death.* New York: McGraw-Hill, 1959.

Fenichel, O. *The Psychoanalytic Theory of Neurosis.* New York: Norton, 1945.

Frankl, V. E. The Will to Meaning. *J. Pastoral Care*, 1956, 12(2).

———. *The Doctor and the Soul.* New York: Knopf, 1957.

———. *From Death Camp to Existentialism.* Boston: Beacon Press, 1959a.

———. Grundriss der Existenzanalyse und Logotherapie (Outline of Existential Analysis and Logotherapy). *Handb. d. Neurosenlehre u. Psychother.* Munich: Urban & Schwarzenberg, 1959b. Vol. 3.

———. Beyond Self-Actualization and Self-Expression. *Existential Psychiat.*, 1960, 1(1), 5–20.

French, T. M. *The Integration of Behavior.* Chicago: University of Chicago Press, 1952, 1954, 1956. 3 vols.

Frenkel-Brunswik, E. A Study of Prejudice in Children. *Human Relations*, 1948, 1, 295–306.

———. Intolerance of Ambiguity as an Emotional and Perceptual Personality Variable. *J. Personal.*, 1949, 18, 108–143.

———. Personality Theory and Perception. In R. R. Blake and

G. V. Ramsey (Eds.), *Perception.* New York: Ronald, 1951.

————, and E. Weisskopf. *Wunsch und Pflicht im Aufbau des menschlichen Lebens* (Desire and Duty in the Structure of Human Life). Vienna: Gerold & Co., 1937.

Freud, S. The Interpretation of Dreams. In *The Standard Edition,* Vol. 4. London: Hogarth Press, 1920.

————. Beyond the Pleasure Principle. In *The Standard Edition,* Vol. 18. London: Hogarth Press, 1920.

————. *New Introductory Lectures.* New York: Norton, 1932.

————. Lines of Distance in Psychoanalytic Therapy (1918). In *The Standard Edition,* Vol. 17. London: Hogarth Press, 1955.

Fries, M. D. Factors in Character Development: Neuroses, Psychoses and Delinquency. *Amer. J. Orthopsychiat.,* 1937, 7, 142–181.

————, and P. J. Woolf. Some Hypotheses on the Role of the Congenital Activity Type in Personality Development. In *The Psychoanalytic Study of the Child,* Vol. 8. New York: International Universities Press, 1953.

Fromm, E. *Man for Himself.* New York: Holt, Rinehart & Winston, 1947.

————. *Sigmund Freud and His Mission.* New York: Harper, 1958.

————. Value, Psychology and Human Existence. In A. E. Maslow (Ed.), *New Knowledge in Human Values.* New York: Harper, 1959.

Fromm-Reichmann, Frieda, *Principles of Intensive Psychotherapy.* Chicago: University of Chicago Press, 1950.

————. Notes on the History and Philosophy of Psychotherapy. In F. Fromm-Reichmann and J. L. Moreno (Eds.), *Progress in Psychotherapy.* New York: Grune & Stratton, 1956.

Gebsattel, V. E. von. Gedanken zu einer anthropologischen Psychotherapie (Reflections on an Anthropological Psychotherapy). *Handb. d. Neurosenlehre u. Psychother.* Munich: Urban & Schwarzenberg, 1959, Vol. 3.

Gibson, J. A Critical Review of the Concept of Set in Contemporary Experimental Psychology. *Psychol. Bull.,* 38, 781–817.

Ginsburg, S. W., and J. L. Herma. Values and Their Relationship to Psychiatric Principles and Practice. *Amer. J. Psychother.,* 1953, 8(3), 546–573.

Glover, E. *The Technique of Psychoanalysis*. New York: International Universities Press, 1958.

Goldstein, K. *The Organism*. New York: American Book, 1939.

Grinker, R. R. On Identification. *Internat. J. Psychoanal.*, 1957, 38(6).

Hall, C. S., and G. Lindzey. *Theories of Personality*. New York: Wiley, 1957.

Hallowell, A. I. The Self and Its Behavioral Environmental Explorations. *Studies in Culture and Communications*, 1954, 2, 106–165.

Harlow, H. F. The Nature of Love. *Amer. Psychologist*, 1955, 13 (12), 673–685.

———. Primary Affectional Patterns in Primates. *Amer. J. Orthopsychiat.*, 1960, 30(4), 676–684.

Hartman, R. S. The Science of Value. In A. H. Maslow (Ed.), *New Knowledge in Human Values*. New York: Harper, 1959.

Hartmann, H. Psychoanalyse und Wertproblem (Psychoanalysis and Value Problem). *Imago*, 1928, 14, 421, 440.

———. *Ego Psychology and the Problem of Adaptation*. New York: International Universities Press, 1958.

———. *Psychoanalysis and Moral Values*. New York: International Universities Press, 1960.

Havighurst, R. J., M. Z. Robinson, and M. Dorr. The Development of the Ideal Self in Childhood and Adolescence. *J. Educ. Res.*, 1946, 40, 241–257.

Hilgard, E. R. The Role of Learning in Perception. In R. R. Blake and G. V. Ramsey (Eds.), *Perception*. New York: Ronald, 1951.

Hollingshead, A. B., and F. C. Redlich. Social Stratification and Psychiatric Disorders. *Amer. Sociological Rev.*, 1953, 18(2).

Horney, Karen. *Our Inner Conflicts*. New York: Norton, 1945.

Hutschnecker, A. A. Personality Factors in Dying Patients. In H. Feifel (Ed.), *The Meaning of Death*. New York: McGraw-Hill, 1959.

Huxley, J. *Religion without Revelation*. New York: New American Library, 1957.

Jahoda, M. *Current Concepts of Positive Mental Health*. New York: Basic Books, 1958.

Jung, C. Wirklichkeit der Seele (The Soul and Death). Translated in H. Feifel (Ed.), *The Meaning of Death*. New York: McGraw-Hill, 1959.

Kardiner, A. *The Psychological Frontiers of Society*. New York: Columbia University Press, 1946.

Karpf, Fay. *American Social Psychology*. New York: McGraw-Hill, 1932.

————. Dynamic Relationship Therapy. *Social Work Technique*, March-April, May-June, July-August, 1937.

Kautsky, G. Reaktionen auf Spielzeug und Person im zweiten Halbjahr (Reactions to Toy and Person in the Second Half Year of Life). Unpublished Ph.D. dissertation, University of Vienna, 1935.

Kelly, G. A. *The Psychology of Personal Constructs*, New York: Norton, 1955. 2 Vols.

Kelman, H. Goals in Therapy. Round Table Discussion. *Amer. J. Psychoanal.*, 1956, 16(1), 3–4.

Kluckhohn, C. Values and Value Orientations in the Theory of Action: An Exploration in Definition and Classification. In T. Parsons and E. A. Shils (Eds.), *Toward a General Theory of Action*. Cambridge, Mass.: Harvard University Press, 1952.

Kluckhohn, F. R. Dominant and Variant Value Orientations. In C. Kluckhohn and H. A. Murray (Eds.), *Personality in Nature, Society and Culture*. New York: Knopf, 1953.

Kubie, L. S. Problems and Techniques of Psychoanalytic Validation and Progress. In E. R. Hilgard, L. S. Kubie, and E. Pumpian-Mindlin (Eds.), *Psychoanalysis as Science*. New York: Basic Books, 1956.

————. Social Forces and the Neurotic Process. In A. H. Leighton, J. A. Clausen, and R. N. Wilson (Eds.), *Explorations in Social Psychiatry*. New York: Basic Books, 1957.

Langfeldt, G. *The Hypersensitive Mind*. Copenhagen: Ejnar Munksgaard, 1951.

LeBon, G. Psychologie des Foules. In A. H. Leighton, J. A. Clausen, and R. N. Wilson (Eds.), *Explorations in Social Psychiatry*. New York: Basic Books, 1957.

Lewin, K. Vorsatz. Wille und Bedürfnis (Intention, Will and Need). In D. Rapaport (Ed.), *Organization and Pathology of Thought*. New York: Columbia University Press, 1951.

Lorand, S. *The Technique of Psychoanalysis*. New York: International Universities Press, 1946.

229

Lowe C. Marshall. Value Orientations—an Ethical Dilemma. *Amer. Psychologist*, 1959, 14(11), 687–693.

Lundberg, G. Semantics and the Value Problem. *Social Forces*, 1948, 114–116.

McLean, H. V. Psychoanalysis as Concerned with the Problem of Values. In J. H. Masserman (Ed.), *Psychoanalysis and Human Values*. New York: Grune & Stratton, 1960.

Marcuse, H. *Eros and Civilization*. Boston: Beacon Press, 1955.

Margenau, H. The Scientific Basis of Value Theory. In A. H. Maslow (Ed.), *New Knowledge in Human Values*. New York: Harper, 1959.

Maslow, A. H. *Motivation and Personality*. New York: Harper, 1954.

————. *New Knowledge in Human Values*. New York: Harper, 1959.

Masserman, J. H. (Ed.), *Psychoanalysis and Human Values*. New York: Grune & Stratton, 1960.

May, R. Historical and Philosophical Presuppositions for Understanding Therapy. In O. H. Mowrer (Ed.), *Psychotherapy*. New York: Ronald, 1953a.

————. *Man's Search for Himself*. New York: Norton, 1953b.

————, E. Angel, and H. F. Ellenberger (Eds.). *Existence*. New York: Basic Books, 1958.

Mead, M., and M. Wolfenstein. *Childhood in Contemporary Cultures*. Chicago: University of Chicago Press, 1955.

Menninger, K. *Theory of Psychoanalytic Technique*. New York: Basic Books, 1958.

Miller, J. G. Unconscious Processes and Perception. In R. R. Blake and G. V. Ramsey (Eds.), *Perception*. New York: Ronald, 1951.

Mittelmann, B. Motility in Infants, Children and Adults, Patterning and Psychodynamics. *The Psychoanalytic Study of the Child*. Vol. 9. New York: International Universities Press, 1954.

Mohr, G. J. Psychoanalysis: Some Present-Day Assessments. In J. H. Masserman (Ed.), *Psychoanalysis and Human Values*. New York: Grune & Stratton, 1960.

Morris, C. *Varieties of Human Values*. Chicago: University of Chicago Press, 1956.

————, B. T. Eiduson, and D. O'Donovan. Values of Psychiatric Patients. *Behav. Sci.*, October, 1960.

Mowrer, O. H. "Sin," the Lesser of Two Evils. *Amer. Psychologist*, 1960, 15(2), 113–118.

Munroe, R. L. *Schools of Psychoanalytic Thought*. New York: Holt, Rinehart & Winston, 1955.

Murphy, G. *Personality*. New York: Harper, 1947.

————. The Cultural Context of Guidance. *Pers. Guide*, 1955, 34, 4–9.

————. *Human Potentialities*. New York: Basic Books, 1958.

Murphy, L. Learning How Children Cope with Problems. *Children*, 1957, 4(4), 132–136.

Mussen, P. H., and J. J. Conger. *Child Development and Personality*. New York: Harper, 1956.

Opler, M. K. *Culture, Psychiatry and Human Values*. Springfield, Ill.: Charles C Thomas, 1956.

Oppenheimer, R. Analogy in Science. *Amer. Psychologist*, 1956, 11, 127–135.

Orlans, H. Some Attitudes toward Death. *Diogenes*, 1957, 19, 72–91.

Parsons, T., and E. A. Shils (Eds.). *Toward a General Theory of Action*, Cambridge, Mass.: Harvard University Press, 1952.

Patterson, C. H. *Counseling and Psychotherapy: Theory and Practice*. New York: Harper, 1959.

Piaget, J. *Dreams and Imitation in Childhood*. New York: Norton, 1951.

————. The Problem of Consciousness in Child Psychology: Developmental Changes in Awareness. In H. A. Abramson (Ed.), *Problems of Consciousness*. New York: Josiah Macy, Jr., Foundation, 1954a.

————. *The Construction of Reality in the Child*. New York: Basic Books, 1954b.

Rapaport, D. (Ed.), *Organization and Pathology of Thought*. New York: Columbia University Press, 1951.

Redlich, F. C. The Concept of Health in Psychiatry. In A. H. Leighton, J. A. Clausen, and R. N. Wilson (Eds.), *Explorations in Social Psychiatry*. New York: Basic Books, 1957.

————. Psychoanalysis and the Problem of Values. In J. H. Masserman (Ed.), *Psychoanalysis and Human Values*. New York: Grune & Stratton, 1960.

Redlich, F. C., and A. B. Hollingshead. *Social Class and Mental Illness.* New York: Wiley, 1958.

Ripin, R. A Study of the Infant's Feeding Reactions during the First Six Months of Life. *Archives of Psych.*, 1930, 116, 38 ff.

Rogers, C. *Client-Centered Therapy.* Boston: Houghton-Mifflin, 1951.

———. Client-Centered Therapy: A Current View. In F. Fromm-Reichmann and J. L. Moreno (Eds.), *Progress in Psychotherapy.* New York: Grune & Stratton, 1956.

Schmideberg, Melitta. A Major Task of Therapy: Developing Volition and Purpose. *Amer. J. Psychother.*, 1961, 15(2), 251–259.

Sears, P. The Pursuit of Self Esteem: The Middle Childhood Years. (In press.)

Seward, G. *Clinical Studies in Culture Conflict.* New York: Ronald, 1958.

———. The Relation between Psychoanalytic "School" and Value Problems in Therapy. (In press.)

Shneidman, E. S., and N. L. Farberow. *Clues to Suicide.* New York: McGraw-Hill, 1957.

Sontag, L. W. The Genetics of Differences in Psychosomatic Patterns in Childhood. *Amer. J. Orthopsychiat.*, 1950, 20, 8.

Sopchak, A. L. Parental "Identification" and "Tendencies toward Disorder" as Measured by the MMPI, *J. Abn. Soc. Psych.*, 1952, 47, 159–165.

Spiegel, J. P. Some Cultural Aspects of Transference and Counter-transference. In J. H. Masserman (Ed.), *Individual and Familial Dynamics.* New York: Grune & Stratton, 1959.

Spitz, R. Hospitalism. In *The Psychoanalytic Study of the Child,* Vol. 1. New York: International Universities Press, 1945.

———. Genèse des Premières Relations Objectales (Development of the First Object Relationships). *Revue Française de Psych.*, 1954.

Stainbrook, E. Some Characteristics of the Psychopathology of Schizophrenic Behavior in Bahian Society. *Amer. J. Psychiat.*, 1952, 109, 330–335.

Standal, S. W., and R. J. Corsini. *Critical Incidents in Psychotherapy.* Englewood Cliffs, N. J.: Prentice-Hall, 1959.

Sterba, R. The Abuse of Interpretation. *Biol. & Pathol. Interpers. Relations,* 1941, 4(1).

————. The Formative Activity of the Analyst. *Internat. J. Psychoanal.*, 1944, 25, 146, 150.

————. Therapeutic Goal and Present-Day Reality. *J. Hillside Hosp.*, 1960, 9(4), 195–217.

Sullivan, H. S. *Conceptions of Modern Psychotherapy.* Washington, D.C.: William Alanson White Psychiatric Foundation, 1947.

Symonds, P. M., with A. R. Jensen. *From Adolescent to Adult.* New York: Columbia University Press, 1961.

Szasz, T. The Myth of Mental Illness. *Amer. Psychologist*, 1960, 15(2), 113–118.

Thompson, C. *Psychoanalysis: Evolution and Development.* New York: Hermitage House, 1950.

Thompson, V. R., and C. H. Hockman. *Behavioral Effects in the Offspring of Rats Subjected to Audiogenic Seizure during the Gestational Period.* Paper read at Proc. East. Psychol. Ass., Atlantic City, March, 1956.

Thorne, F. C. Principles of Personality Counseling, *J. Clin. Psychol.*, 1950.

Tinbergen, N. Social Releases and the Experimental Method Required for Their Study. *Wilson Bull.*, 1948, 60, 6–51.

Tolman, E. A Psychological Model. In T. Parsons and E. A. Shils (Eds.), *Toward a General Theory of Action.* Cambridge, Mass.: Harvard University Press, 1952.

Waddington, C. H. *The Ethical Animal.* London: Allen & Unwin, 1960.

Weil, A. P. Some Evidences of Deviational Development of Infancy and Early Childhood. In *The Psychoanalytic Study of the Child*, Vol. 2. New York: International Universities Press, 1946.

————. Clinical Data and Dynamic Considerations in Certain Cases of Childhood Schizophrenia. *Amer. J. Orthopsychiat.*, 1953, 23(3).

————, A. Alpert, and P. B. Neubauer. Unusual Variations in Drive Endowment. In *The Psychoanalytic Study of the Child*, Vol. 2. New York: International Universities Press, 1946.

Weiss, F. A. Goals in Therapy. Round Table Discussion. *Amer. J. Psychoanal.*, 1956, 16(1), 15–18.

Wheelis, A. *The Quest for Identity.* New York: Norton, 1958.

Whitehorn, J. C. Understanding Psychotherapy. In F. Fromm-

Reichmann and J. L. Moreno (Eds.), *Progress in Psychotherapy*. New York: Grune & Stratton, 1956.

Winker, J. B. Age Trends and Sex Differences in the Wishes, Identifications, Activities and Fears of Children. *Child Dev.*, 1949, 20(4), 191–200.

Wolberg, L. R. *The Technique of Psychotherapy*. New York: Grune & Stratton, 1950.

Wolff, W. *Values and Personality*. New York: Grune & Stratton, 1950.

Wylie, R. C. *The Self Concept*. Lincoln, Neb.: University of Nebraska Press, 1961.

Name Index

235

List of Patients' Pseudonyms

List of Biographies

Subject Index

239

Guilt feelings, 94, 111, 113, 120, 143, 167

Habit acquisition, 43
Habits, persisting, 75
Happiness, 87, 117, 147
Harmony, inner, 87, 117
Hate, 92, 120
Health, as value, 34, 117, 143
Healthy functioning, 5, 174
  of baby, 83
  development of, 110 f, 111 ff, 121 ff
  process of, 66
  value development in, 131 ff
Heredity, 63, 67
Holistic point of view, 173 f
Homeostasis, 54, 82
Honesty, 33, 39, 44, 45, 93
Hostility, 174
Hope, 160, 174
Hopeful confidence, 159
Human existence, concept of, 116
Human life, interpretation of, 2
Human personality, 14
Human potentialities, 116
Humanism, ethical, 40
Humanistic ethics, 58
Hypersensitivity, 73, 86, 169 f
Hypnosis, Freud's use of, 182 f, 186 f
Hypothesis, of child, 158
  of thinker, 158

Id, 51, 66, 179
  impulses of, 52
Ideal, superego, 95, 100
  ego, 95
Ideals, conscious, 81
  incorporation of, 94
  own, 100
  self-determination to, 65, 98
Identities, different, 89
Identity, 5, 55 ff, 66 f, 148 f
  adolescents', 103
  beginning of, 155
  choice of, 94
  concept of, 154 ff
  conflicts, 218

cultural, 55
dawning of, 89
development of, 154 f
ego, 55
individual, 55
  and life cycle, 80
negative, 37
personal, 55
sexual, 106
  and value, 154 ff
Identification, 4, 22, 53 ff, 82, 90 f, 148, 156
  by name, 110
  with obligations, 110
  problem of, 200 ff
Identifying conviction, 159 ff
Ideology, of culture, 47
  of patient, 46
  and psychoanalysis, 179
  of psychotherapy, 195
Illness, bodily, 130
  concept of, 180
  and social help, 186
Imitation, 94 f
  of infant, 82, 86
  of mother, 90
Imitative identification, 85
Imitative responsiveness, 95
Impulses, biological, 81
  social, 61
  socio-biologic, 61
Incentive, linking of, 214
  new, 219
Inclinations, natural, 42
Incorporation, 53
Inculcation, 210
Indecision, 6, 125
Independence, 103
Individual, and environment, 69 f
  himself, 64
Individual differences, 72 ff
Infancy, early, 86
Infant, directivity of, 83
  hypersensitive, 169
  observations of, 74
  self of, 83
  trust of, 72
Infant behavior, 73
Infants, 84
  monkey, 85